BITCOIN INVESTING FOR BEGINNERS

Unlocking Financial Freedom with Digital Gold and Cryptocurrency

Mark Swanson

Table of Contents

Introduction

In the early days, when Bitcoin was just another tech buzzword, I was having a casual dinner with a friend who couldn't stop talking about digital currencies. I remember nodding politely, all the while thinking, "This will never catch on." Fast forward, and not only has Bitcoin caught on, but it has exploded into a phenomenon that reshaped my view of financial investments and the very perception of money. This transformation from skeptic to advocate wasn't overnight, but it was profound—and opened my eyes to the untapped opportunities in the digital currency space.

This book is crafted around the central thesis that Bitcoin is far more than a speculative bubble; it's a revolutionary technology that offers not only substantial financial opportunities but also a chance to rethink our relationship with money. In this book you will discover Bitcoin not only as an asset but also as an innovation that may well define the future of finance.

The purpose of "Bitcoin for Beginners: How to Invest and Profit from Cryptocurrency" is simple: to break down the complexities of cryptocurrency investing, focusing particularly on Bitcoin. It's tailored for you—adults who may have heard about Bitcoin on the news or from a friend but don't have a background in technology or finance—and are looking for a clear, reliable guide to understanding and investing in Bitcoin.

What sets this book apart is its commitment to clarity and practicality. Drawing from my own journey into the world of Bitcoin, I strive to present information that is not only informative but also actionable. You won't get lost in technical jargon here. Instead, you'll find straightforward explanations accompanied by real-world advice that you can apply to your own investment decisions.

The structure of the book is designed to guide you step by step. We'll start with the origins and basics of Bitcoin, delve into different investment strategies, explore how to manage risks, and finally, look towards the future of Bitcoin. Each section builds upon the last, ensuring that when you finish the book, you'll have a comprehensive understanding of the subject.

I encourage you to not just read this book but to actively engage with it. Reflect on the discussion questions, try out the exercises, and apply what you learn to your personal financial situation. This is not just about investing in Bitcoin—it's about empowering yourself with knowledge to make informed financial decisions.

As we embark on this journey together, remember that understanding and investing in Bitcoin could be one of the most empowering financial decisions you make. My passion for financial education is the core of this book, and I am here to guide you through each step of your Bitcoin investment journey.

Let's decode the world of cryptocurrency and unlock new opportunities for growth and independence together. Welcome to "Bitcoin for Beginners."

Chapter 1

Understanding Bitcoin and Cryptocurrency

Have you ever stopped to wonder what really lies behind the hype about Bitcoin? You might have caught fragments of it on the news—jaw-dropping stories of early investors turning into overnight millionaires or ominous predictions about a digital bubble set to burst. But beyond these headlines, there's a transformative financial landscape that's been slowly redefining the very essence of money and transactions. In this chapter, we'll peel back the layers of what might just be the most significant financial revolution of our time, and no, it's not just about making a quick buck. It's about understanding a new way of thinking about currency, investment, and our economic autonomy.

What is Bitcoin? The Genesis of Digital Currency

Definition and Origin

In 2009, amidst the ashes of the most severe fiscal disasters since the Great Depression, an entity—or possibly a group—under the pseudonym Satoshi Nakamoto introduced Bitcoin to the world. This wasn't just another digital currency; it was the first decentralized digital currency. Fundamentally, Bitcoin was envisioned as an electronic cash system that was completely peer-to-peer, which meant it could simplify transactions between individuals without the need for a central authority, such as a bank or government. This radical approach to money was a direct response to the distrust in traditional financial institutions at the time, with many feeling that these entities had played fast and loose with their responsibilities and the public's trust.

Key Characteristics

Bitcoin introduces several radical features that set it apart from traditional currencies. First, it's decentralized, which means it's not controlled by any single entity. The consequences of this are enormous, as it places the power of managing currency back into the hands of the people. Secondly, Bitcoin has a limited supply— there will only ever be 21 million Bitcoins in existence. This scarcity is similar to precious metals such as gold, which have historically been used as a hedge against inflation and the devaluation of currency. Additionally, Bitcoin is divisible, meaning you can own and transact fractions of a Bitcoin (up to eight decimal places), making it accessible for small and large transactions alike. Lastly, it's portable, as Bitcoin can be sent anywhere in the world via an internet connection without the need for intermediaries and is often cheaper and faster than traditional international wire transfers.

Bitcoin's Intent

The original intent of Bitcoin was to provide an alternative to the fiat currency system by creating a method of exchange that was secure, transparent, and efficient. Distinct from traditional currencies, which can be manipulated and are often devalued by governments and financial institutions, Bitcoin operates on a model of mathematical certainty. It's built on a technology called blockchain, which ensures that every transaction is recorded in a public ledger and visible to all but is tamper-proof and secure. This system not only reduces the possibility of fraud but also eliminates the need for costly intermediaries, thereby democratizing financial transactions and giving control back to the individual user.

Cultural Impact

Bitcoin's emergence has sparked a global conversation about the future of money. It has challenged the monopoly of national currencies and central banks and has inspired a wave of technological innovation in finance that continues to this day. Other cryptocurrencies have since emerged, each offering unique solutions to different challenges, but all building on the foundational principles introduced by Bitcoin. Moreover, Bitcoin has influenced discussions on financial privacy, sovereignty, and inclusion, pushing these vital issues to the forefront of global economic conversations.

Reflection Section

To better grasp the revolutionary impact of Bitcoin, reflect on the following questions:

- How do you currently perceive the reliability and stability of traditional banks and financial institutions?

- In what ways can a decentralized currency like Bitcoin change your personal financial autonomy?

- What are the potential benefits and challenges of a currency that has a limited, predetermined supply?

Through these reflections, you can begin to understand not only the functions of Bitcoin but also its profound implications on a personal and global scale. Remember them as we continue, keep these thoughts in mind, and consider how the shift towards digital currencies might influence not just your wallet but also the broader economic landscape.

Decoding Cryptocurrency: From Blockchain to Bitcoin

Imagine walking into a room where a group of people, each holding a notebook, records every transaction you make. Each note is cross-checked for accuracy, and no single person controls the record. Instead, everyone in the room has a copy of the same book. This is a simplified glimpse into how blockchain technology, the bedrock of cryptocurrencies like Bitcoin, functions. The blockchain is fundamentally a digital ledger that is maintained by a network of multiple nodes (computers), which makes it decentralized. Every 'block' in the chain is comprised of several transactions, and each time a new one occurs, a record of the transaction is added to each participant's ledger. It's this infrastructure that underpins Bitcoin and allows it to operate securely and transparently without the need for a central authority.

Now, let's delve deeper into how blockchain powers Bitcoin. You can think of blockchain as the foundation upon which Bitcoin is built. If you want to send Bitcoin to another person, the transaction details are broadcast to a network of nodes, the computers participating in the Bitcoin network. These nodes take the information and validate the transaction using a set of cryptographic rules. This process involves miners, who compete to solve complex mathematical problems that validate the transactions; the first miner to unravel the problem will add a new block to the blockchain. This is known as the consensus mechanism, and it's crucial because it ensures that each transaction is confirmed by multiple nodes independently, securing the network from tampering and fraud.

The beauty of blockchain doesn't end with Bitcoin. Its potential applications stretch far beyond cryptocurrency. For instance, consider smart contracts, self-executing contracts with the terms directly written into code, or supply chain management, where blockchain can offer a transparent and unalterable record of product journeys from manufacturer to consumer. These applications underscore blockchain's versatility and capacity to impart efficiency and security in various domains, demonstrating its utility in automating and securing complex processes without the need for a central authority.

Blockchain's technological significance in the realm of cryptocurrency cannot be overstated. It's revolutionary because it eliminates the need for trust in financial transactions. In traditional finance, a transaction will rely heavily on third parties like credit card companies or banks to verify the exchange of money. Blockchain technology disrupts this model by allowing people to make direct transactions with confidence, knowing that the record of their exchange is secure and unchangeable. This aspect is particularly transformative in environments where the reliability of financial institutions might be questionable or where they are non-existent. By democratizing access to secure financial transactions, blockchain is not just a technical innovation; it's a facilitator of financial inclusion and autonomy.

How Bitcoin Works: The Science of Cryptocurrencies

Let's peel back the curtain on how Bitcoin actually functions under the hood. Envisage yourself wanting to send Bitcoin to a friend as a gift. You initiate the transaction by entering the amount of Bitcoin you want to send and your friend's digital wallet address. This is where things get interesting. Every Bitcoin wallet comes with two keys: a public key, which you can think of as a mailbox, and a private key, which acts much like a key to that mailbox. Your friend's public key is used to deposit the Bitcoins, but it's the private key that's crucial because it allows them to access and use the Bitcoins you send. This pair of keys ensures that the transaction is secure. Only the person with the correct private key can access the Bitcoins sent to a specific public key, safeguarding against unauthorized access.

Once you've initiated the transaction, it doesn't just float straight over to your friend. It first needs to be verified and recorded on the blockchain. This is where miners come into play, as they use powerful computers to resolve intricate mathematical problems that validate your transaction. This process is known as proof-of-work. It serves a dual purpose: securing the network from fraudulent transactions and creating new Bitcoins. When a miner successfully solves the mathematical puzzle, this adds a 'block' of transactions to the blockchain. This is no small feat; hence, the network rewards miners by giving them new Bitcoins. This reward halves approximately every four years and is known as the 'halving,' which is why Bitcoin is often compared to precious metals, such as gold—it gets harder and more resource-intensive to mine over time.

Security in Bitcoin goes beyond just the transaction mechanism. Cryptographic techniques are the bedrock of its security features. Bitcoin uses a specific type of cryptography known as the SHA-256 hash function, which turns transaction information into a series of numbers and letters that is virtually impossible to predict. This protects the integrity of your transaction by making it almost impossible for anyone to alter the transaction data. Each block on the blockchain comprises its unique hash and also that of the previous block, creating a link between them. This chain of hashes is what makes the blockchain secure and immutable. If someone attempts to alter a transaction, it changes the hash of the block. Since the blocks are linked, altering one hash would require altering all subsequent hashes, which is computationally impractical.

Now, consider the decentralized nature of Bitcoin's network. Instead of having a central point of control, Bitcoin's ledger is distributed across a network of nodes, each having a replica of the complete blockchain and working to maintain its integrity and accuracy. When a new block is added to the blockchain, each node independently verifies it against the existing blockchain. If a majority of nodes agree that the new block is valid, it is accepted into the blockchain. This decentralization not only enhances security but also increases transparency and makes Bitcoin resistant to censorship. If there's ever a disagreement about a transaction (known as a fork), the blockchain can split into two paths. One path follows the new, contested rules, while the other continues under the old rules, allowing the community to decide which blockchain to continue to use based on consensus, ensuring that the network remains democratic and resilient.

Understanding these processes illuminates why Bitcoin is often hailed as a revolutionary financial technology. It's not merely about the potential monetary gains; it's about the empowerment that comes from having a secure, efficient, and transparent way to transact without the need for old-style financial intermediaries. This technology could potentially reshape the global economic landscape, making transactions quicker, cheaper, and more accessible to people around the world who are currently outside the reach of traditional banking services. As we continue to explore the implications and applications of Bitcoin, it becomes clear that its true power lies not just in its ability to generate wealth but in its potential to change how we think about and engage with the financial systems of the world.

Comparing Bitcoin and Traditional Banking

When you think about traditional banking, images of massive buildings, long lines, and heaps of paperwork might come to mind. Now, imagine an alternative where transactions are as easy as sending an email without the need for a brick-and-mortar institution acting as the middleman. This is where Bitcoin steps into the picture, challenging centuries-old banking practices with its unique approach to managing transactions. The differences between Bitcoin and traditional banking are stark, primarily revolving around the concepts of privacy, transaction speed, international transfers, and user autonomy.

Privacy in traditional banking is a complex issue; banks are required to collect personal information, ostensibly to protect against fraud, but also make your financial activity an open book to various agencies by default. Bitcoin offers a different approach. Transactions are recorded on a public ledger, yes, but the identities of the parties involved are represented only by their wallet addresses—random strings of numbers and letters. This pseudonymity allows users a degree of privacy that's hard to find in standard financial systems. Moreover, the speed of transactions with Bitcoin contrasts sharply with traditional banking, where transfers can take days to clear, especially if crossing national borders. Bitcoin transactions can be confirmed in as rapidly as ten minutes and, once added to the blockchain, are considered secure and irreversible.

International transfers with Bitcoin also offer a distinct advantage over traditional methods, which can be costly and laden with red tape. Bitcoin simplifies the process, allowing direct transfers without the need for currency exchange or third-party intervention. This not only cuts down on fees but also on the time it takes to send money across borders. It's no wonder that people from countries with unstable currencies or restrictive financial systems find Bitcoin particularly appealing. Lastly, Bitcoin places a great degree of autonomy in the hands of its users. Without the need for a central authority, individuals have complete control over their own digital assets. This means no arbitrary limits on transactions, no exorbitant fees for certain types of transfers, and no risk of asset seizure by corrupt or financially unstable governments.

However, as much as Bitcoin presents advantages over conventional systems, it's not without its challenges. Scalability remains a significant issue. Bitcoin's network currently handles only a fraction of the transactions per second as compared to traditional credit card networks. Efforts to improve this through various means, including the Lightning Network and Segregated Witness (SegWit), are ongoing, but the problem is far from solved. Volatility is another challenge. The cost of Bitcoin can swing wildly within a short period, influenced by factors like regulatory news, market sentiment, and technological developments. This volatility can be a barrier for its adoption as a daily currency rather than just an asset for speculation.

Furthermore, regulatory acceptance varies widely from one jurisdiction to another, affecting everything from Bitcoin's legality to how it's taxed. Countries like Japan have embraced cryptocurrency, providing clear regulatory frameworks that help integrate it into daily financial activities. Others remain skeptical, imposing strict regulations or outright bans that complicate Bitcoin's adoption and use. These challenges highlight the complex landscape that Bitcoin must navigate to gain broader acceptance and fulfill its potential as a valid alternative to traditional financial systems.

Looking ahead, the potential for Bitcoin to either complement or disrupt traditional banking remains a topic of much debate. On the one hand, its advantages in terms of transaction speed, cost, and user autonomy present a compelling case for its integration into the existing financial ecosystem. Banks are already exploring ways to harness blockchain technology for faster and more secure transactions. On the other hand, Bitcoin's decentralization and ability to operate outside the traditional finance system pose a disruptive threat to established banking institutions, potentially diminishing their role in the global economy.

As we continue to explore the intricacies of Bitcoin and its place in the financial world, it's clear that its journey is still in its early stages. The coming years will undoubtedly bring further challenges, opportunities, and innovations that will inevitably shape the future of both Bitcoin and traditional banking. How these two systems will interact, compete, or integrate is still unfolding, and the implications for investors, consumers, and financial professionals are vast and varied. As with any emerging technology, the landscape is dynamic, and the potential for transformation is enormous.

Key Bitcoin Terminologies Explained

Navigating the world of Bitcoin can sometimes feel like learning a new language. From 'Satoshi' to 'wallets,' understanding these terms is critical for anyone looking to participate in Bitcoin, whether it's for investing purposes or simply to better understand this digital currency revolution. Let's break down some of these essential terms in a way that's easy to grasp.

The lowest Bitcoin unit is called a 'Satoshi' after its mysterious creator, Satoshi Nakamoto. One Satoshi is to Bitcoin what a penny is to a dollar—only much, much smaller. To put it in perspective, one Bitcoin is equivalent to 100,000,000 Satoshis. This divisibility is part of what makes Bitcoin suitable for micro-transactions, unlike traditional currencies, which are often limited by physical coins or small denomination bills.

When we talk about a 'wallet' in Bitcoin terms, we're not referring to a physical wallet you carry in your pocket, but rather a digital one. This wallet is where you store your Bitcoin. There are two main types of wallets: digital wallets, which are software programs that can store your Bitcoin online, on your computer or mobile device, and hardware wallets, which are physical devices that keep your Bitcoin stored offline. Hardware wallets are often considered more secure because they aren't connected to the internet, which shields them from hacking attempts and other online vulnerabilities.

Understanding 'hash rate' is critical to grasping how Bitcoin mining works. The hash rate measures the performance of the miners—the individuals and companies who contribute the computing power necessary to maintain the Bitcoin network and process transactions. In more technical terms, the hash rate is the speed at which a miner's hardware operates as it tries to solve the cryptographic puzzles that add new blocks to the blockchain. A higher hash rate increases a miner's chance of finding the next block and receiving the Bitcoin reward. This rate not only reflects the health and security of the Bitcoin network but also affects how quickly transactions are processed.

'Nodes' are the individual computers that connect to the Bitcoin network, each hosting a copy of the entire blockchain. These nodes play a crucial role in the consensus process, working to verify the legitimacy of transactions and blocks. They're the backbone that keeps the Bitcoin network decentralized and secure. Each node independently checks transactions against the existing blockchain, rejecting those that don't conform to the network rules. This decentralized verification process is fundamental to Bitcoin's security and trustworthiness.

A 'fork' in the Bitcoin world occurs when there is a change to the blockchain software that creates two different versions of the history. This usually happens when the community behind Bitcoin is divided about the best way to move forward. Forks can be planned as part of the network's upgrade process, or they can be contentious, leading to a permanent split and creating a new cryptocurrency.

Let's now discuss 'public and private keys.' These are part of the cryptography that Bitcoin uses to secure transactions. Each Bitcoin wallet may contain several private keys, which are saved in the wallet file and are mathematically connected to all Bitcoin addresses created for the wallet. Essentially, your private key is your digital identity for Bitcoin transactions. It's what you use to sign transactions to prove you own the Bitcoins associated with your address, and you must keep it secure. If someone obtains access to your private keys, they can spend your Bitcoin. On the other hand, the public key is derived from the private well and can be shared with anyone. It's like your bank account number that you'd give to someone who needs to send you money.

Lastly, we have 'altcoins' and 'ICOs.' Altcoins, or alternative coins, are cryptocurrencies other than Bitcoin. Many altcoins are built on the basic framework provided by Bitcoin but aim to improve or offer different capabilities. Examples include Ethereum, Ripple, and Litecoin, each with its own unique features and uses. Initial Coin Offerings, or ICOs, are a fundraising mechanism used mainly by startup companies offering products and services related to cryptocurrency and blockchain space. ICOs can be a risky investment because they're relatively unregulated, but they can also provide the potential for significant returns, similar to early investments in startups.

Understanding these terms not only enriches your knowledge of how Bitcoin operates but also enhances your ability to participate in conversations about cryptocurrency. Whether you're discussing investment opportunities, exploring the technology, or simply satisfying your curiosity, a solid grasp of these concepts is invaluable. As you continue to explore Bitcoin and perhaps even start to interact with the system, keep these definitions in mind. They'll serve as your guideposts in the dynamic and ever-evolving landscape of cryptocurrency.

Chapter 2

The Historical Context and Economic Impact

Have you ever wondered how money evolved from simple barter systems to the complex digital currencies we use today? It's a fascinating journey that not only reflects technological advancements but also shifts in societal needs and values. In this chapter, we'll explore the tapestry of monetary evolution and carve out a space for Bitcoin in the grand scheme of things. This exploration isn't just academic; understanding where Bitcoin fits into the history of money can give us insight into its potential future and the role it might play in reshaping our global financial landscape.

A Brief History of Money and Where Bitcoin Fits

From Barter to Digital: Tracing the Evolution of Money

The story of money is as old as civilization itself. In the beginning, there was barter—simple, straightforward trade. I give you something you need, and in return, you give me something I need. However, as communities expanded and trade grew more complex, carrying around the items you wanted to trade became impractical. Enter commodity money—goods that held universal value, like salt or gold, used to represent wealth. These were portable, durable, and, importantly, divisible, making trade easier and more efficient.

Fast forward a few centuries, and we see the introduction of metal coins and, eventually, paper money—each innovation driven by the need for more convenient, scalable methods of trade. Paper money, a representation of value stored somewhere else, marked a significant shift. It was a promise, a bearer of trust that the paper could be exchanged for something of equal value. As societies continued to evolve, so too did their financial needs, which led to the creation of credit cards and electronic banking. These digital transactions enabled commerce on a scale previously unimaginable, connecting global economies in real time.

The Emergence of Digital Currency

As the internet began to dominate the landscape of communication and commerce, it was only a matter of time before digital currencies emerged. These were currencies born of the digital age, meant to simplify transactions in an increasingly online world. Initially, digital currencies were centralized and created by companies as tokens for use within specific online communities. However, they were limited by the trust placed in these central authorities—trust that was not always upheld.

Bitcoin, introduced in 2009, revolutionized this concept by creating a decentralized digital currency. For the first time, digital money could be sent directly from one person to another without going through a bank or payment gateway. This was made possible by blockchain technology—a decentralized record that chronicles all transactions across a network of computers. The implications were profound, as this not only minimized the risk of fraud but also democratized financial transactions, removing the control from central institutions and placing it back into the hands of individuals.

Bitcoin's Unique Place in Monetary History

Bitcoin stands out in the history of money for its ability to solve the double-spend problem without the need for a trusted authority. In traditional digital transactions, a central authority had to verify that each unit of currency hadn't been spent twice. With Bitcoin, this verification is decentralized, spread across a network of nodes that see and verify each transaction. This not only enhances security but also aligns with a growing desire for transparency and autonomy in financial dealings.

Implications for the Future of Money

As we look to the future, Bitcoin's potential to influence the global financial system continues to grow. It challenges traditional banking infrastructures, offers new forms of financial inclusivity, and may even redefine what we consider as 'money.' Could Bitcoin or other cryptocurrencies replace traditional money? It's a possibility worth considering. More likely, however, is a future in which digital and traditional forms of money coexist, each serving unique needs within the global economy. This coexistence could lead to a more diversified, resilient, and democratic financial system globally.

In navigating this evolution, remember that the steps we take now — how we regulate, adopt, and integrate technologies like Bitcoin — will shape the financial landscapes of tomorrow. As you reflect on Bitcoin's place in the tapestry of monetary history, consider how its principles of decentralization and transparency could influence not only financial systems but also broader societal structures. Imagine a world where financial inclusivity is the norm and the barriers to economic participation are dramatically reduced. This isn't just theoretical; it's a potential future that grows more tangible with each transaction recorded on the blockchain.

As we continue to explore Bitcoin's role and influence, keep in mind the broader implications of this digital revolution. The shift toward decentralized currencies could herald a new era of economic interaction, one in which power is distributed more evenly and the rules of engagement are rewritten for the betterment of all.

Bitcoin and the Concept of Decentralization

Decentralization is a term that often pops up in discussions about Bitcoin, but what does it really mean, especially in the context of finance and technology? At its core, decentralization refers to the distribution of power away from a central authority. In financial systems, this means moving control from traditional institutions like banks and governments to a distributed network, typically using technology. Bitcoin embodies this concept through its blockchain technology, where every transaction is verified by multiple nodes (computers) across the globe rather than by a single central entity. This significant attribute of Bitcoin is not just a technical detail; it's the philosophical backbone that makes Bitcoin uniquely positioned to redefine aspects of our financial systems.

The contrast between decentralized systems like Bitcoin and centralized financial systems is stark. Centralized systems operate through central authorities such as banks, which control transaction verifications, the creation of new units of currency, and the overarching rules of their operation. These systems have been the foundation of our economies for centuries; however, they come with drawbacks. Centralization can lead to inefficiencies, such as slow transaction times and higher costs due to intermediaries. Moreover, they can be prone to corruption and mismanagement—risks that are borne by the users. On the other hand, decentralized systems like Bitcoin allow transactions to be verified by a consensus among participants, dramatically reducing the need for intermediaries. This can lead to speedier transaction times and lower costs. Additionally, the decentralized nature of Bitcoin minimizes the risks of corruption and central points of failure.

However, while decentralization has its advantages, it also impacts financial autonomy in profound ways. By reducing reliance on traditional financial institutions, Bitcoin allows individuals to have more control over their financial transactions. You're no longer bound by the fees, terms, and conditions imposed by banks. More importantly, this shift can empower individuals in underbanked or unstable regions to access financial services without the need for a physical bank. This aspect of Bitcoin is transformative, offering a level of financial autonomy that was previously unattainable for many.

Despite these benefits, decentralization comes with its own set of challenges. Regulatory issues are a significant hurdle. Without central oversight, it can be difficult for governments to enforce financial regulations such as anti-money laundering (AML) and know-your-customer (KYC) standards. This can make Bitcoin a potential tool for illegal activities. Furthermore, the decentralized nature of Bitcoin could lead to fragmentation in financial policies if not integrated thoughtfully within existing monetary systems. Addressing these challenges requires innovative regulatory approaches that balance the need for control with the benefits of decentralization. Regulators might need to develop new frameworks that recognize the unique attributes of decentralized systems without stifling their growth.

Another challenge is the potential for misuse. Without centralized control, bad actors could potentially manipulate transaction verifications or take advantage of the anonymity provided by cryptocurrencies like Bitcoin for nefarious purposes. However, the community-driven nature of Bitcoin has led to the development of various protocols that enhance security and transparency. For instance, continuous updates to the Bitcoin network protocol aim to address vulnerabilities as they arise. Moreover, the transparency of the blockchain allows transactions to be publicly tracked, adding a layer of accountability that is often absent in traditional systems.

In navigating these challenges, the role of community consensus in the development and governance of Bitcoin becomes crucial. Unlike centralized systems, where decisions are made by a few, decisions in Bitcoin's network are made by consensus, offering a democratic approach to financial governance. This not only helps mitigate risks but also ensures that changes to the network reflect the collective interest of its users.

As we explore the broader implications of Bitcoin's decentralization, it's clear that this concept is reshaping not just the technical landscape of transactions but also the very notion of financial autonomy and security. Decentralization challenges the traditional paradigms of financial governance and opens up new possibilities for user empowerment and systemic resilience. While the road ahead is fraught with challenges, the potential for positive change makes it an exciting area of development in the evolution of money.

How Bitcoin Challenges the Fiat Currency System

When you hold a dollar, euro, or any other fiat currency, you're essentially holding a piece of a country's economic system. The value of this currency hinges mainly on the government's ability to maintain it; however, this system isn't without its flaws. Fiat money, which is money without intrinsic value that a government has declared to be legal tender, is vulnerable to inflation. This often occurs when governments print more money to cover their debts, effectively diluting the value of existing money. Moreover, fiat currencies are inextricably linked to the political and economic stability of the governments that issue them. In times of political unrest or poor economic management, the value of fiat money can fluctuate wildly.

In stark contrast, Bitcoin stands as a currency untethered from governmental oversight. Its decentralized nature means no single entity can dictate its value or arbitrarily decide to increase its supply. Bitcoin's protocol caps its total supply at 21 million coins, a stark contrast to government-sanctioned currencies, which may be printed at the whim of policymakers. This integral scarceness is similar to precious metals such as gold, which have historically retained value due to their limited nature. This feature of Bitcoin is x particularly appealing to those who wish to hedge against inflation. Unlike fiat currencies, which can lose value over time, Bitcoin's design inherently avoids this downside, which makes it a deflationary asset.

The real-world implications of this are profound, especially in countries that experience hyperinflation. Consider Venezuela, where hyperinflation reached 1,000,000% in 2018, rendering the local currency, the bolivar, nearly worthless. In such economies, Bitcoin offers an attractive alternative. It provides a stable source of value and means of transaction outside the rapidly depreciating local currency. In Zimbabwe, another country plagued by severe inflation, Bitcoin has become so in demand that it has traded at rates significantly higher than in more stable economies. This high premium reflects its perceived value as a stabilizing force, where locals turn to Bitcoin to conserve their savings and engage in commerce without the constant fear of their money losing value overnight.

Moreover, Bitcoin is inherently resistant to censorship and seizure. Each transaction is recorded on a blockchain, a distributed ledger that no single party controls. This architecture not only makes Bitcoin transactions nearly impossible to censor but also protects against seizure. In regions where political unrest or economic instability is prevalent, this aspect of Bitcoin is particularly critical. For instance, during political protests in Nigeria in 2020, government authorities targeted the bank accounts of activists. In response, many turned to Bitcoin and other cryptocurrencies to fund their activities, circumventing governmental control and ensuring the continuation of their efforts. This resistance to censorship and seizure not only makes Bitcoin an attractive financial tool in such contexts but also underscores its role in promoting financial sovereignty.

In these ways, Bitcoin stands not merely as an alternative to fiat currencies but as a critique of the system itself. It challenges the conventional financial and political structures that have governed how money is created, valued, and exchanged for centuries. As Bitcoin continues to gain traction, it forces us to rethink the very fabric of economic policy and monetary control. Whether it will replace fiat currencies entirely remains to be seen, but its impact on how we think about and use money is undeniable. As we navigate this evolving landscape, Bitcoin remains a key player in the dialogue about not only our economic futures but also about the balance of power between governments and the governed.

Understanding Bitcoin's Role in Global Finance

In the realm of global finance, Bitcoin is making waves not just as a speculative asset but as a functional currency that's reshaping how we think about and engage in international transactions. The traditional banking system, with its layers of intermediaries and hefty fees, often makes moving money across borders a costly and time-consuming endeavor. Bitcoin, on the other hand, streamlines this process significantly. By utilizing blockchain technology, Bitcoin allows for transfers that bypass traditional financial intermediaries, offering a direct route from sender to receiver. This not only slashes transaction fees but also drastically reduces the time it takes for funds to be transferred across national borders. Imagine sending money from the U.S. to Australia and having it arrive in minutes rather than days and at a fraction of the cost of a wire transfer or remittance service. This efficiency makes Bitcoin an attractive option for businesses and individuals looking to operate on a global scale, ensuring faster and cheaper transactions that can keep pace with the speed of international commerce.

Moreover, Bitcoin is significantly impacting the world of remittances, where immigrants send money back to their home countries. Old-style payment channels often come with high fees, which can be burdensome for individuals sending money home regularly. Bitcoin and other cryptocurrencies offer a much cheaper alternative with fees that are typically a small fraction of what would be paid through conventional remittance services. The lower cost will make a substantial difference in the lives of families receiving these funds, ensuring that more money actually makes its way into the hands of those who need it rather than being lost to transaction fees. Furthermore, the accessibility of Bitcoin transactions via smartphones means that these transfers can be made without the need for a bank account, which is an essential benefit in regions where banking services are limited or non-existent.

The incorporation of Bitcoin into existing financial systems is also progressing, with several banks and financial institutions beginning to recognize the potential benefits of cryptocurrency. Some are exploring the use of Bitcoin for transaction services, while others are investing in cryptocurrency exchanges or creating their own digital currency platforms. This integration is a testament to Bitcoin's growing legitimacy and its potential to complement traditional financial services. By partnering with existing financial institutions, Bitcoin can leverage the strengths of both the new and old financial systems, creating a hybrid model that offers more flexibility and efficiency than could be achieved by either one alone. Such partnerships can help connect the traditional financial world and the expanding crypto economy, facilitating smoother transactions that incorporate the best aspects of both worlds.

Finally, Bitcoin holds tremendous potential for enhancing financial inclusion worldwide. Anyone can create a Bitcoin wallet using only a smartphone and internet access and start receiving and sending funds. This accessibility is particularly crucial for the unbanked populations of the world, who may lack access to traditional banking services but can still participate in the global economy through Bitcoin. The implications of this are profound, offering economic empowerment to millions who have previously been marginalized by the conventional financial system. By providing these individuals with the tools to save, invest, and transact on a global scale, Bitcoin is not just a currency or an investment; it's a tool for social change, enabling greater participation in the economic processes that shape our world.

As Bitcoin continues to evolve and become part of the global financial landscape, its role as a catalyst for economic change becomes increasingly apparent. Whether it's transforming how we think about international transactions, reducing the cost of remittances, partnering with traditional financial institutions, or promoting financial inclusion, Bitcoin is proving to be a significant force in the redefinition of global finance. As we move forward, the continued adaptation and integration of Bitcoin will likely unlock new possibilities for efficiency, inclusivity, and innovation in financial services, reshaping the economic landscape in ways that are currently hard to imagine.

The Philosophy Behind Bitcoin and Economic Freedom

The seeds of Bitcoin were sown in a soil rich with libertarian ideas, emphasizing individual liberty, skepticism of authority, and the importance of privacy. The creators and early adopters of Bitcoin were heavily influenced by these ideas, viewing the cryptocurrency as a tool to reduce or eliminate the role of government in personal transactions. This philosophical backbone sets Bitcoin apart from traditional currencies and embeds it with a potential for societal change that goes beyond mere financial transactions.

Bitcoin was born following the 2008 financial crisis—a time when trust in global financial institutions and governments was notably eroding. The creators of Bitcoin envisioned a system where monetary transactions no longer required approval from banks or governments, thus sidestepping the pitfalls of political and economic mismanagement seen in the fiat currency systems. This vision is encapsulated in Bitcoin's decentralized nature, where transactions are verified by a network of peers rather than a central authority.

This not only enhances privacy by masking the identities of the parties involved behind cryptographic keys but also aligns with the libertarian value of minimizing state control and surveillance.

Moreover, Bitcoin's potential as a tool for economic empowerment is immense. By circumventing traditional financial institutions, it offers individuals unprecedented control over their financial dealings. For someone in a developing country without access to a bank, Bitcoin can provide a gateway to participate in global transactions and access services previously out of reach. This empowerment extends to combating inflation and financial instability often seen in countries with less stable economic systems. By providing a more stable store of value than their national currencies, Bitcoin gives individuals a way to preserve their wealth independently of their government's economic decisions.

Despite its potential, Bitcoin is not without its critics. Some argue that its emphasis on anonymity makes it an ideal conduit for illegal activities, such as money laundering or funding terrorism. However, these concerns are often countered by the benefits Bitcoin offers in terms of financial privacy and security. While it's true that Bitcoin, like any tool, can be misused, it also provides legitimate users with protection from identity theft and financial fraud by keeping their personal information private. Furthermore, the transparency of the blockchain ledger ensures that all transactions are traceable, which can actually aid law enforcement in tracking down illicit activity more effectively than with traditional cash transactions.

Looking to the future, the widespread adoption of Bitcoin could significantly alter the landscape of global economic systems. Imagine a world where financial transactions are seamlessly conducted across borders without the need for currency exchange or third-party verification. This could lead to a more interconnected and efficient global economy, with lower transaction costs and higher accessibility. The decentralization of financial power could also lead to greater economic democratization, where individuals have a greater say in their economic destinies without undue influence from centralized authorities.

This vision of the future is not without challenges. The volatility of Bitcoin, regulatory hurdles, and the technological complexities of blockchain technology are significant barriers to its widespread adoption. However, as the technology matures and more people become aware of its benefits, these challenges may be overcome, leading to a more decentralized and equitable global financial system.

Reflecting on these points, Bitcoin offers more than just an alternative to traditional financial systems. It embodies a philosophy of economic freedom and empowerment, challenging us to rethink the role of money in society. As we continue to explore Bitcoin's capabilities and address its challenges, we may find that its most significant impact is not on our wallets but on our very concepts of freedom and autonomy in an increasingly digital world.

As we wrap up this exploration of Bitcoin's philosophical underpinnings, we see a digital currency that is much more than a technological novelty. It is a manifestation of a desire for greater financial freedom and a challenge to the traditional power structures that govern our economic lives. Moving forward, the journey of Bitcoin will undoubtedly be fascinating, filled with debates, innovations, and, perhaps, a redefinition of money itself. In the next chapter, we delve deeper into the practicalities of Bitcoin—how to acquire, store, and use it effectively—guiding you through the technical aspects of handling Bitcoin while considering its broader implications.

Chapter 3

Getting Started with Bitcoin

Imagine standing at the threshold of a new financial universe where the control of your money is entirely in your hands, free from the grip of traditional banking systems. That's the promise of Bitcoin, and it all begins with setting up your very first Bitcoin wallet. Think of this wallet not just as a tool but as your personal gateway to buying, storing, and using Bitcoin. It's where the magic happens, and today, I'll guide you through every step to create and secure your Bitcoin wallet, ensuring you start on the right foot in your Bitcoin adventure.

Setting Up Your First Bitcoin Wallet

Choosing the Right Wallet

When it comes to storing your Bitcoin, you have a few options, each with its own set of benefits and considerations. There are three main types of wallets to choose from: software wallets, hardware wallets, and paper wallets.

Software wallets are apps or programs that you can download to your computer or phone and are an easy way to access and manage your Bitcoin, making them ideal for everyday use and small amounts of money. However, they are only as secure as the device they are on, so if your device is hacked, there's a risk your Bitcoin could be stolen.

On the other hand, a hardware wallet is a physical device designed specifically for storing cryptocurrency. It looks a bit like a USB drive and is considered one of the safest options available. A hardware wallet will keep your personal keys offline and away from potential online vulnerabilities, offering an excellent balance between security and convenience for larger amounts of Bitcoin or long-term holdings.

Paper wallets are exactly what they sound like: your Bitcoin private and public keys printed out on a piece of paper. While they are completely safe from hackers, they come with their own risks. If the paper is lost, damaged, or destroyed, so are your Bitcoin. Paper wallets are best for those who want to store Bitcoin away for a long time and can ensure the safekeeping of the paper.

Choosing the right wallet depends largely on how you plan to use your Bitcoin. If you're planning on using Bitcoin for daily transactions, a software wallet might be the way to go. If you're looking at Bitcoin as a long-term investment, a hardware wallet provides the security you'll need. And for those considering Bitcoin as a legacy to hold onto for many years, a paper wallet—while requiring careful handling—could be the perfect choice.

Step-by-Step Wallet Setup

Let's walk through setting up a software wallet, as it's the most common choice for beginners. First, choose a reputable wallet provider. Look for one with a strong track record of security and user-friendly features. Once you've downloaded the app or software, the next step is creating your account. This usually involves setting a strong password and, in some cases, linking your email or mobile phone for security purposes.

Navigating the user interface is your next step. Spend some time familiarizing yourself with the layout. Look for features like the 'send' and 'receive' buttons, your transaction history, and your current balance. Most wallets will also have a section for managing your security settings—don't skip this.

Backup and Recovery

Backing up your wallet is crucial. Most wallets provide you with a recovery phrase when you set them up. This phrase should consist of 12 to 24 words and is used to restore your wallet if your computer or phone is lost or damaged. Write this phrase down on paper, then place it in a safe place where only you can access it. Never store your recovery phrase digitally or share it with anyone else.

Initial Security Measures

To protect your wallet from unauthorized access, strong passwords are a must, but don't stop there. Enable two-factor authentication (2FA) if your wallet supports it. This adds additional security by requiring not just your password but also a code sent to your phone or email when a transaction is made or if any important change is made to your account.

Other security measures include regularly updating your wallet software and keeping the devices on which your wallet is installed secure. Remember, the safety of your Bitcoin wallet is entirely in your hands, and taking these steps can help ensure the security of your digital currency.

By following these steps, you can set up and secure your first Bitcoin wallet, positioning yourself to safely participate in the exciting world of Bitcoin. Whether you're buying your first fraction of a Bitcoin or preparing to manage a more significant investment, these foundational steps are critical to your success in the cryptocurrency space.

Secure Purchasing of Bitcoin: A Step-by-Step Guide

Navigating the world of Bitcoin exchanges can feel like a maze, especially when you're trying to pinpoint the perfect one for your needs. Selecting a reputable Bitcoin exchange is your first crucial step toward buying Bitcoin securely. In this vast sea of options, focus on a few key aspects: security features, user reviews, fee structure, and regulatory compliance. A well-reputed exchange usually boasts robust security measures, such as two-factor authentication, cold storage options for customer funds, and insured custodial services. Take the time to read reviews from other users to gauge their experiences—both positive and negative—and pay attention to the fee structure, as well, since fees can vary significantly between exchanges and can affect your buying power. Lastly, ensure the exchange complies with regulations, particularly those related to anti-money laundering (AML) and know your customer (KYC) policies. Not only does this add a layer of security, but it also ensures the exchange is operating under strict guidelines that protect its users.

Once you've chosen an exchange that feels right, setting up an account is your next step. This process typically starts with registering your basic information, followed by a more detailed identity verification process. The KYC procedures are crucial as they help avert fraud and confirm that only legitimate users are trading on the platform. You'll probably need to provide a government-issued ID, proof of address, and possibly a recent photo to verify your identity. While this might seem cumbersome, it's a critical step in safeguarding your investments.

Now, let's talk about making your first Bitcoin purchase, which can be thrilling but also a bit daunting. Most exchanges offer a straightforward process to buy Bitcoin, usually starting with depositing fiat currency—such as US dollars (USD,) euros (EUR,) or British pounds sterling (GBP)—into your account. Once your funds are deposited, you're ready to buy. When placing an order, you'll find options like 'market orders' and 'limit orders.' A market order buys Bitcoin instantly at current market price, whereas a limit order lets you set a specific price at which you want to buy. The latter can be helpful if you expect the price to drop and want to lock in a lower purchase price. Understanding this often helps you make informed decisions that align with your investment strategy.

After purchasing Bitcoin, the paramount step is transferring your new digital asset to a personal wallet, reinforcing the security of your investment. While keeping Bitcoin on an exchange is convenient for trading, exchanges are more vulnerable to hacks. Transferring your Bitcoin involves locating the 'withdraw' or 'send' function on the exchange, entering your personal wallet's address, and specifying the amount of Bitcoin you wish to transfer. Double-check the address before confirming the transaction to avoid irreversible mistakes. Additionally, be mindful of transaction fees, which are required to process and confirm your transaction on the blockchain. These fees can vary based on how busy the network is at the time of your transfer, so it's wise to consider these costs when planning your purchase.

By walking through these steps carefully, you ensure that your initiation into the Bitcoin world is not only exciting but also secure. Remember, each step, from choosing an exchange to transferring funds to your wallet, builds upon the last, fortifying the security and integrity of your Bitcoin transactions. As you become more familiar with these processes, you'll find yourself navigating them with greater confidence and precision, which will pave the way for more advanced ventures in your Bitcoin journey.

Understanding and Protecting Your Private Keys

When you first dive into the world of Bitcoin, you'll often hear about the critical importance of "private keys." But what exactly are these, and why do they play such a pivotal role in the security of your Bitcoin assets? Think of private keys as the most guarded part of your Bitcoin wallet—the part that allows you to unlock and control your Bitcoin. Essentially, a private key is a sophisticated form of coding that allows a user to access their cryptocurrency. It's a unique string of characters known only to you, much like a super-secure password. Each private key is mathematically linked to a wallet address (your public key) but is not publicly disclosed. It's what keeps your Bitcoin secure and ensures that only you can access it.

The generation of these private keys is a marvel of modern cryptography. When you set up a new wallet, the software randomly generates a private key, which in turn generates a public key. The relationship between the two is irreversible—you can easily create a public key from a private key, but not the other way around. This one-way street is vital because it keeps your private key secure even though your public key is shared with the world. Understanding this mechanism is essential because the security and integrity of your Bitcoin transactions depend heavily on the confidentiality of your private key.

The risks associated with exposing your private key are severe. If someone else obtains it, they can transfer all of your Bitcoin to another account—and this action is irreversible. The most common ways private keys are exposed include phishing attacks, where scammers trick you into revealing your key; malware, which can log your keystrokes or steal wallet files; and even physical theft or loss. Each of these scenarios will leave your digital assets vulnerable, highlighting the need for stringent security measures.

To manage and store your private keys effectively, adhering to best practices is non-negotiable. One of the most secure methods is using a hardware wallet. These devices store your private keys offline, isolated from online vulnerabilities such as hackers and viruses. More importantly, they allow you to make transactions online while keeping your private keys away from your computer or smartphone. Avoid storing significant amounts of Bitcoin in wallets that are continuously connected to the internet (often referred to as 'hot wallets'). Instead, consider using 'cold storage' options like paper wallets or hardware devices for large amounts or long-term holdings.

Another critical practice is never to store your private keys in plain text files or take digital photographs of paper wallets. Instead, write them down on paper and store them in a secure location, such as a safety deposit box. Multiple backups in geographically diverse locations can also safeguard against the risk of physical damage or loss.

So, what should you do if your private keys are lost or compromised? First, if you suspect that your private key has been stolen but you still have control over your wallet, transfer your funds to a new wallet immediately using a newly generated private key. If you've lost your private key, recovery can be challenging and sometimes impossible. This is why many wallets provide a mnemonic recovery phrase—a series of words generated at the setup of your wallet. This phrase, which can be used to regenerate your private key, should be written down and stored as securely as the key itself.

When dealing with private keys, the predominant theme is clear: the security of your Bitcoin hinges on the integrity and confidentiality of your private keys. By understanding their role, actively protecting them, and preparing for potential emergencies, you can ensure that your digital assets remain under your control, safeguarding your investments and giving you peace of mind in the unpredictable realm of cryptocurrency.

Common Mistakes to Avoid as a Bitcoin Beginner

Navigating the exciting yet intricate world of Bitcoin can be a rewarding experience, but this also comes with its own set of pitfalls that can trip up even the most enthusiastic beginner. Understanding some common oversights and errors can help you manage your digital assets more securely and with greater confidence. Let's explore some of these typical missteps so you can avoid them.

The importance of robust security practices cannot be overstated in the realm of cryptocurrency. A common oversight many newcomers make is the reuse of passwords on numerous platforms. This can lead to a domino effect where one compromised account can lead to breaches across all your accounts, including your Bitcoin wallet. Always use unique, strong passwords for each account, and consider using a reputable password manager to keep track of them. Additionally, while it may seem like a small step, enabling two-factor authentication (2FA) on all accounts that support it, including your Bitcoin wallet and exchange accounts, provides an extra layer of security that can thwart attempts at unauthorized access. Moreover, always ensure that you are using secure and private networks when accessing your Bitcoin-related accounts. Using Wi-Fi in a public place, for instance, is an opportunity for cyber thieves who can intercept unsecured data transmitted across such networks.

Another common pitfall in the Bitcoin sphere is falling victim to scams and phishing attempts. The cryptocurrency world, with its relative anonymity and significant financial stakes, is ripe for a variety of scams. Phishing attacks, where scammers attempt to trick you into giving them your personal information or login credentials, are particularly prevalent. Always double-check the URLs of sites you visit, and don't ever click on suspicious links from emails or messages. Be wary of too-good-to-be-true investment schemes that promise high returns with little to no risk. Remember, in the financial world, high returns always come with high risks, and this is especially true in the volatile cryptocurrency market. Educating yourself about common Bitcoin scams and staying informed about new threats can significantly reduce your risk of falling victim to cybercriminals.

Understanding the volatile nature of Bitcoin prices is crucial for every newcomer. The cryptocurrency market is known for its rapid price fluctuations, which can be exhilarating but also daunting. A common mistake is to make investment decisions based on panic or hype, which can lead to buying high and selling low—the opposite of the general investment strategy goal. Instead of reacting to market volatility with panic, a more measured approach involves doing thorough research and setting clear, strategic objectives for your investments. Decide how much of your portfolio you want to assign to Bitcoin and stick to this limit. It's also wise to avoid checking the price too frequently, which can prevent knee-jerk reactions to short-term market movements. Instead, focus on long-term trends and think about Bitcoin's potential in your investment portfolio.

Lastly, the legal and tax implications of owning and trading Bitcoin often go overlooked by beginners eager to dive into the market. The regulatory landscape for cryptocurrency is still evolving, and it varies significantly by country. Failing to comply with legal and tax obligations can involve serious consequences, including hefty fines and penalties. Take the time to understand the laws and regulations regarding Bitcoin in your jurisdiction. This might include reporting your transactions and holdings on your tax returns or adhering to specific legal guidelines about the use of cryptocurrency. Consulting with a financial advisor or a tax professional who is knowledgeable about cryptocurrency can provide you with tailored advice that will help you stay compliant and within the law.

By steering clear of these common mistakes, you can navigate the Bitcoin waters more safely and effectively. Remember, every step in managing your Bitcoin—from setting up your wallet to making informed investment decisions—should be approached with caution and knowledge. As you continue to learn and grow in your Bitcoin journey, these practices will not only protect your investments but also enrich your experience in the cryptocurrency world.

Verifying and Tracking Bitcoin Transactions

Understanding how to verify and track Bitcoin transactions is like learning to read the fine print of your financial activities, ensuring you're fully aware and in control. Each transaction on the Bitcoin network is recorded in a public ledger known as the blockchain. This transparency is Bitcoin's forte, allowing anyone to check the status of any transaction at any time. To verify a transaction, you can use a blockchain explorer. These are websites that provide detailed information about all transactions and blocks on the Bitcoin blockchain. By entering your transaction ID—a unique identifier assigned to each transaction—you can view its confirmation status and the number of times it has been confirmed by the network.

Confirmations are essential because they indicate how many blocks (additional transactions) have been added to the blockchain since your transaction was recorded. Generally, more confirmations mean higher security; most services require at least six confirmations for a transaction to be considered entirely secure.

Transaction fees play a pivotal role in the Bitcoin ecosystem, acting as an incentive for miners to include transactions in their blocks. These fees are not fixed and may vary widely depending on several factors, including the data size of the transaction and network demand. Higher fees may encourage faster confirmation during periods of congestion, as miners will prioritize transactions with higher fees. Deciding on an appropriate fee can sometimes feel like a balancing act. Most Bitcoin wallets provide a fee estimator that suggests a fee based on current network conditions and transaction size, which can guide you to set a fee that balances cost with confirmation speed. It's also helpful to check the current average transaction fees using a blockchain explorer or dedicated fee tracking websites to ensure you're not overpaying.

Keeping track of your Bitcoin holdings is crucial, especially as your portfolio grows. There are several tools and methods that can help with this, such as portfolio trackers and applications that allow you to monitor the value of your Bitcoin holdings in real time, along with other investments. Many of these trackers can link directly to your wallets and exchange accounts to automatically update your balances and transaction history. For those who prefer a more hands-on approach, accounting software that supports cryptocurrencies can be invaluable. These programs can help you record transactions, calculate gains and losses, and even prepare financial reports, thus simplifying the management of your Bitcoin finances.

Maintaining privacy in your Bitcoin transactions can be challenging but is crucial, especially given the public nature of the blockchain. One fundamental practice is to use a new address for each transaction. Most modern wallets automatically generate a new address for you for every transaction, which can help obscure which transactions are connected to you. For enhanced privacy, consider using a privacy-focused wallet or services that mix your Bitcoins with others, breaking the traceable path on the blockchain. However, be cautious with these services as they can sometimes operate in legally grey areas.

By mastering these aspects of Bitcoin transactions, you empower yourself with the knowledge to navigate the crypto waters safely, keeping your transactions secure, your fees appropriate, and your privacy intact. With these skills, you can confidently monitor and manage your digital assets, ensuring your Bitcoin journey is both rewarding and secure.

As we wrap up this chapter on getting started with Bitcoin, you've equipped yourself with the essential tools and knowledge to set up and secure a wallet, make educated purchases, understand the importance of private keys, and avoid common pitfalls. With this foundation, you're ready to delve deeper into the strategic aspects of Bitcoin investing, which we will explore in the next chapter. Here, we'll shift our focus from the mechanics of handling Bitcoin to making informed decisions that align with your financial goals.

Chapter 4

Investment Strategies and Managing Risks

Imagine stepping into the world of Bitcoin investing with a roadmap in your hands, one that not only shows you where to go but also when to take action. That's what this chapter aims to provide—a guide to understanding the rhythms and cues of the Bitcoin market that can significantly enhance your investing strategy. Let's start with a deep dive into the market cycles of Bitcoin, explore the impact of global events, and learn how to harness tools for sentiment analysis and timing techniques. These insights will not only bolster your confidence but will also refine your investing decisions, helping you to navigate the ups and downs of the market with greater ease.

Assessing the Right Time to Invest in Bitcoin

Understanding Market Cycles

The Bitcoin market experiences cycles that can provide insightful cues for investment decisions, like any other financial market. These cycles are characteristically composed of four phases: accumulation, uptrend, distribution, and downtrend. During the accumulation phase, prices are generally flat as knowledgeable investors begin to buy, anticipating future value increases. This phase is often marked by a sense of uncertainty among average investors. Next, the uptrend phase (also known as the 'markup' phase) begins, where prices start rising steadily and public interest grows. This is often where you'll see media buzz and hear stories of people making substantial gains.

Following the uptrend, the market enters the distribution phase. Here, traders and investors start to sell their holdings, taking profits from the increases during the uptrend. Prices may still rise on average, but fluctuations begin to appear, showing the first signs of volatility. Finally, the downtrend phase sets in, where prices fall, sometimes as dramatically as they rose. This can be generated by various factors, including market saturation, external economic factors, or a change in investor sentiment. Understanding these phases can help you recognize whether Bitcoin is currently undervalued or overpriced, guiding your decisions on when might be a good time to buy or sell.

Impact of Global Events

Global events significantly impact Bitcoin's price, reflecting its interconnection with worldwide economic and political landscapes. For instance, regulatory announcements regarding cryptocurrency, such as a new government policy to either support or restrict the use of Bitcoin, often lead to immediate and significant market reactions. Economic crises, trade wars, or geopolitical events can also influence Bitcoin prices. For example, during times of economic instability, such as the financial crisis in Greece in 2015, more people turned to Bitcoin, pushing prices up. On the other hand, announcements of regulatory crackdowns, such as those in China in 2017, can cause prices to plummet.

Sentiment Analysis

Sentiment analysis involves gauging the mood or opinions of the market participants, often through analyzing data from several sources, including social media, news articles, and market indicators. Tools like sentiment indicators or social media analytics software can help you tap into the market's mood and provide clues about potential price movements. For example, a sudden spike in negative sentiment on social media platforms can sometimes precede a drop in Bitcoin prices, as it may indicate growing investor anxiety or pessimism.

Timing Techniques

One effective strategy to manage investment timing in such a volatile market is dollar-cost averaging (DCA). This technique means investing a fixed amount at regular intervals in Bitcoin, regardless of the price—a strategy that will help reduce the impact of instability on the overall purchase. The idea is to build up the investment over time, smoothing out the purchasing price across the highs and lows of the market's cycle. Another timing technique is to buy during periods of consolidation—when prices are relatively stable—before the next market moves higher. This requires keeping a keen eye on market trends and being prepared to act when the time seems right.

Through understanding market cycles, the impact of global events, sentiment analysis, and strategic timing, you can improve your ability to make informed investment decisions in the Bitcoin market. These elements provide a framework within which you can assess the market's current condition and its potential future movements, helping you to buy and sell with greater confidence and theoretically better outcomes. As we navigate through these concepts, remember that investing in Bitcoin, like any investment, involves a degree of risk. The key is to make well-informed decisions, drawing on a broad range of tools and information to guide your investment strategy.

Long-term vs. Short-term Bitcoin Investment Strategies

When you step into the Bitcoin investment arena, it's like choosing between sprinting or running a marathon. Both styles have their unique rhythms and rewards, and knowing the nuances of each can significantly impact your financial outcome. First, let us define what long-term and short-term investments generally look like in the Bitcoin context. Long-term investment, often referred to as "HODLing" in the crypto community, means holding onto Bitcoin with the expectation that its value will increase over years or even decades. This strategy is less about daily fluctuations and more about the big picture, counting on the idea that despite its volatility, Bitcoin will continue to gain value over time. Short-term investment, on the other hand, is more like day trading, where investors buy and sell Bitcoin based on short-term market movements. These can last from a few minutes to several months, depending on the strategy.

The pros and cons of each are worth considering. Long-term holding has the potential for substantial returns, as history has shown significant price increases for Bitcoin over several years. This strategy requires less time and attention on a daily basis, as you won't be reacting to every dip or peak. However, this requires a lot of patience and a strong nerve to ride out the inevitable ups and downs. Emotional stress is often lower, as long-term investors are generally not swayed by short-term market volatility. On the flip side, short-term trading can also be lucrative, offering the possibility of profiting from Bitcoin's unpredictability by capitalizing on market highs and lows—a strategy that requires a deep understanding of market trends and a lot of time to monitor market movements. It can be highly stressful, as money can be lost as quickly as it was gained.

To bring these strategies to life, consider the real-life examples of two Bitcoin investors. Let's start with Sarah, a long-term holder who bought her first Bitcoin in 2014 when the price was around $800. Despite the dramatic fluctuations, including the peak near $20,000 in 2017 and the subsequent drop below $4,000 in 2018, she held onto her investment. By 2021, her patience paid off when the price soared to new heights, significantly increasing her initial investment. Contrast this with Mike, a short-term trader who started trading Bitcoin in late 2019. By carefully analyzing market trends and sentiment, he made multiple trades over weeks and months, capturing profits during the volatility of the 2020 and 2021 market surges. While both faced different challenges and stress levels, their tailored strategies worked well for each individual's financial goals and risk tolerances.

Choosing between these strategies involves a careful assessment of your financial goals, risk tolerance, and time availability. If you're looking at Bitcoin as a way to build wealth over many years, perhaps even as part of your retirement plan, then long-term investing might be for you. This approach will be less stressful as it doesn't require constant market monitoring. However, if you enjoy the thrill of trading and can afford the time and the emotional rollercoaster of short-term market movements, then short-term strategies might be more up your alley. It's also worth considering a mixed approach, where you hold a core amount of Bitcoin long-term but allocate a smaller portion for short-term trading.

When navigating through these investment strategies, remember that each investor's journey is unique. What works for one person might not work for another. The key is to understand the characteristic risks and benefits of each strategy and choose one that aligns with your financial goals and lifestyle. Whether you choose to sprint or run the marathon, or even a combination of both, the world of Bitcoin investing is ripe with opportunities for those who are prepared. As you explore these strategies, continue to refine your approach based on your experience and developing market conditions. This adaptive strategy can help ensure that your investment decisions are sound, responsive, and, in due course, more rewarding.

Risk Management in Bitcoin Investments

Navigating the turbulent waters of Bitcoin investing requires more than just knowing when to buy and sell. Effective risk management is crucial in order to safeguard your investment from the unexpected twists and turns in the cryptocurrency market. Let's unpack some fundamental risk management concepts that every Bitcoin investor should understand and implement.

Risk management in the context of Bitcoin investing involves strategic techniques to minimize potential losses while maximizing potential gains. One of the key concepts here is the risk/reward ratio, which helps you assess whether the potential reward of a Bitcoin investment outweighs the risk involved. This ratio is calculated by dividing the amount you will lose if the price moves against you (the risk) by the potential gain (the reward) if the price moves in your favor. A favorable risk/reward ratio is typically greater than 1:1, meaning the potential gains should outweigh the potential losses. Another vital concept is position sizing, which involves determining how much of your total investment capital to allocate to a particular investment. Proper position sizing is crucial as it helps you spread your risk and avoid significant damage from a single trade.

Additionally, using a stop-loss order can be a game changer. A stop-loss order is one placed with your broker to purchase or sell once the asset has reached a specific price. It is designed to limit an investor's loss on a position in a security. By placing a stop-loss order, you can automatically sell off your Bitcoin if its price dips to a level you have predefined as unacceptable, thus preventing further losses.

Identifying the risks associated with Bitcoin investing is just as critical as knowing how to manage them. Their volatility is perhaps the most well-known risk. The price of Bitcoin has been known to wildly fluctuate over short periods, influenced by factors such as market sentiment, regulatory news, and changes in the technological landscape. Regulatory changes are another significant risk. As governments around the world grapple with how to handle cryptocurrencies, new regulations can have sudden and profound effects on the market. For instance, an announcement of stricter regulations can lead to price drops, while favorable regulations can cause prices to surge. Technically, Bitcoin is not immune to vulnerabilities. The technology underlying Bitcoin is still relatively new, and unforeseen bugs or flaws in the system could potentially be exploited, leading to loss of funds.

Mitigating these risks starts with diversification. Don't put all your eggs in one basket! While Bitcoin might be the star of your portfolio, consider diversifying into other cryptocurrencies or blockchain projects to spread your risk. This move will protect your portfolio from being too exposed to the fortunes (or misfortunes) of a single asset. Using secure storage solutions is also paramount—use hardware wallets, which store your private keys offline and protect from computer viruses and hackers. Keeping yourself informed cannot be overstressed. Stay updated on technological and regulatory developments in the cryptocurrency world. This can help you to anticipate potential issues and adapt your strategy accordingly, possibly saving you from substantial losses.

Creating a personalized risk management plan involves several steps. Start by defining clear investment objectives. What are you hoping to achieve with your Bitcoin investment? Are you looking for short-term gains, or are you in it for the long haul? If you understand your goals, this will help you control how much risk you are willing to take. Next, assess your risk tolerance, which measures your willingness to endure the market's volatility and uncertainty. Your risk tolerance will certainly affect how much of your portfolio you might want to allocate to Bitcoin versus other less volatile investments. Once you have a clear understanding of your objectives and risk tolerance, establish mechanisms to monitor and adjust your investment plan as necessary. This will probably involve setting up regular reviews of your portfolio, keeping an eye on market developments, and being poised to adapt your strategy in response to new information.

By integrating these risk management techniques into your Bitcoin investing strategy, you can protect your investments from unexpected downturns and improve your chances of long-term success. Risk management will not eliminate risk entirely—that's impossible in any investment—but understand and manage the risks in a way that aligns with your overall investment goals. With a solid plan in place, you can approach Bitcoin investing with confidence, knowing that you are prepared to handle whatever the market throws your way.

Diversifying Your Investment Portfolio with Bitcoin

When you think about diversifying your investment portfolio, you're essentially looking at ways to spread out your investment risks and increase your potential for returns. This is where Bitcoin can play a pivotal role. As a non-correlated asset, Bitcoin has shown that its market movement is not typically aligned with traditional financial assets like stocks or bonds. This unique attribute makes it a valuable tool for diversification, helping to reduce overall investment risk while providing a hedge against inflation and economic instability. For instance, during times when traditional markets may be underperforming due to economic downturns or inflationary pressures, Bitcoin's price has sometimes moved independently or even appreciated, offering a buffer that can help stabilize your portfolio's value.

Diversifying within the cryptocurrency space itself can also enhance your investment strategy. Beyond Bitcoin, the world of cryptocurrencies is rich with alternatives, including various altcoins and tokens, each offering different technologies, use cases, and potential benefits. For example, Ethereum, with its smart contract functionality, presents a different set of opportunities and risks compared to Bitcoin. There are also stablecoins, which are pegged to traditional currencies like the US dollar, providing stability in a portfolio that includes more volatile crypto assets. Furthermore, the burgeoning field of DeFi, or decentralized finance, offers yield-generating opportunities through mechanisms such as staking, lending, and liquidity provision, which are not typically found in other traditional financial products.

Another layer of diversification can be achieved through Bitcoin derivatives, such as futures and options. These financial instruments allow you to hedge your bets or speculate on Bitcoin's price movements without actually holding the currency. For instance, if you believe Bitcoin's price will go down, you could buy a put option or sell a futures contract as a form of insurance against losses in your Bitcoin holdings. This strategy can be very useful in managing the risks associated with Bitcoin's price volatility.

Balancing traditional investments with cryptocurrency holdings is more of an art than a science. It involves understanding not only the potential returns and risks of each asset class but also how they interact within your overall portfolio. A well-rounded portfolio characteristically includes a mix of assets—stocks, bonds, real estate, and, increasingly, cryptocurrencies like Bitcoin. Each of these plays a role in achieving your financial goals, whether it's capital appreciation, income generation, or preservation of capital. For instance, bonds offer regular income and are generally safer, while stocks and Bitcoin may provide higher growth potential but with increased risk. Real estate offers tangible asset ownership and can also provide income through rent.

Monitoring and rebalancing your portfolio are crucial practices to make sure that your investments continue to align with your financial goals and risk tolerance. This involves regularly reviewing your asset allocation to confirm it remains optimal. For example, if Bitcoin's value has increased significantly, it might represent a larger proportion of your portfolio than you initially intended, increasing your overall risk. In such cases, you might decide to sell some of your Bitcoin to rebalance your portfolio back to its target allocation. Tools and platforms that provide comprehensive views of your assets and automated rebalancing can help simplify this process, allowing you to easily stay on top of your investments.

By incorporating Bitcoin and other cryptocurrencies into your diversified investment portfolio, you're not only spreading your risk but also positioning yourself to capitalize on the growth potential of some of the most dynamic and innovative asset classes in the market today. As with any other investment, the key to success lies in careful planning, ongoing education, and staying adaptable to the ever-changing financial landscape.

Using Technical Analysis to Guide Bitcoin Investments

As you dip your toes into the vast ocean of Bitcoin investing, understanding the currents—market trends and patterns—can significantly enhance your navigation skills. This is where technical analysis comes into play, serving as a compass to guide your investment decisions. Technical analysis primarily involves the study of price, volume, and past market data to forecast future price movements. This method is built on the assumption that all up-to-date market information is reflected in the price, which follows identifiable patterns or trends that are likely to repeat over time.

One of the basic concepts in technical analysis is the identification of trends. A trend can indicate the general direction in which the market is moving and can be upward, downward, or sideways. Recognizing these trends early can help you make decisions about when to buy or sell. For example, in a strong upward trend, it might be advantageous to hold onto your Bitcoin, whereas a downward trend might signal a good time to sell or wait for a more favorable entry point. Closely tied to trends are support and resistance levels, which are predetermined points on the price chart where the forces of supply and demand meet. Support levels are prices at which buyers consistently enter the market, preventing prices from further deterioration, while resistance levels are the prices at which the sellers repeatedly cap price increases.

The volume of trades is another critical indicator in technical analysis as it provides clues about the strength of a price move. High volumes often confirm the trend direction, as they suggest that a large number of assets are being traded. For instance, if the Bitcoin price breaks above a known resistance level on high volume, this is generally taken as a confirmation that the price might continue to rise as buyer interest is strong.

Several key indicators are invaluable to refine your technical analysis. Moving averages are among the most popular and easy-to-use tools. They streamline the price data to create a single flowing line, making it easier to identify the direction of the trend. The Simple Moving Average (SMA) and the Exponential Moving Average (EMA) are two types you might consider. The Relative Strength Index (RSI) is an additional powerful tool that can be used to calculate the speed and change of prices using a scale of 0 to 100—an asset is typically considered to be overbought when the RSI is above 70 and oversold when it's below 30, potentially signaling upcoming reversals. The Moving Average Convergence Divergence (MACD) is a more sophisticated tool that helps track momentum by displaying the relationship between two moving averages of a cryptocurrency's price. Lastly, Bollinger Bands provide a visual of the price volatility; they widen during periods of high volatility and contract when volatility decreases.

Chart patterns may also play a critical role in technical analysis, as they help traders predict future market movements. Patterns like the 'head and shoulders' or 'double top' can indicate trend reversals, while 'triangles' or 'flags' can signal the continuation of a trend. Being able to spot these patterns early will give you a substantial advantage in your trading strategy.

While technical analysis can be incredibly powerful, it's most effective when used in conjunction with fundamental analysis, which involves evaluating a cryptocurrency's value based on external factors and intrinsic value. This holistic type of approach can provide a more comprehensive view of the market, combining the 'what' and 'why' of market movements. For instance, if technical analysis suggests a bullish trend but recent regulatory changes are likely to impact the cryptocurrency negatively, it might be wise to temper your actions with this fundamental insight.

By mastering technical analysis, you equip yourself with the tools to make more informed decisions about your Bitcoin investments. This method won't guarantee success, as markets can be unpredictable, but it will provide a solid framework for understanding market dynamics and managing potential risks. As you grow more comfortable with these concepts, you'll find yourself better able to anticipate and react to market movements, potentially leading to more successful investment outcomes.

As we conclude this exploration of technical analysis, remember that the key to effective Bitcoin investing lies in a balanced approach that considers both market trends and underlying factors. The insights gained from technical analysis are valuable, but they are just one part of the broader investment landscape. Looking ahead, the next chapter delves into the exciting realm of Bitcoin technologies, where innovation continues to reshape the possibilities within the cryptocurrency world. This exploration will not only broaden your understanding of what drives Bitcoin but also enhance your ability to navigate its future developments.

Chapter 5

Advanced Bitcoin Technologies

Diving into the world of Bitcoin mining might feel like you're stepping into a digital gold rush era, where instead of shovels and pans, miners arm themselves with powerful computers and a sharp understanding of cryptography. This chapter will unravel the fascinating process of Bitcoin mining by exploring each step, from the role of miners to the sophisticated evolution of mining technology that keeps the Bitcoin network robust and secure.

An In-depth Look at Bitcoin Mining

Imagine a worldwide competition where millions of participants solve complex puzzles 24/7, and the winners get rewarded in digital gold—Bitcoin. This is Bitcoin mining in a nutshell, but let's break it down further to understand the intricacies involved. Mining is shown to be the backbone of the Bitcoin network. Miners utilize powerful computers to solve cryptographic puzzles, and the first to reach the solution may add a new block of transactions to the Bitcoin blockchain. This process not only creates new bitcoins but also verifies and secures transactions without the need for a central authority.

Mining Process Explained

The mining process begins when transactions are broadcast to the network. Miners collect these transactions and start forming a block. Individual blocks contain a cryptographic hash of the preceding block, which links them in a chain, hence the term 'blockchain.' To add a block to a chain, the miner has to find the solution to a complex cryptographic puzzle related to the hash of the previous block. This puzzle involves guessing a number called a nonce. The correct nonce, combined with the data in the block, produces a hash that meets the network's required standards, known as the difficulty level. This level adjusts every 2016 blocks, roughly every two weeks, to ensure that the time to find a block remains about ten minutes, regardless of how many miners are competing.

Role of Mining Pools

Given the competitive nature of mining and the sheer computational power required, an individual miner often finds it challenging to compete with larger mining operations. This is where mining pools come into play—a group of miners who combine their computing power to increase their chances of solving cryptographic puzzles and earning rewards. When a pool succeeds, the reward is distributed among its members based on the amount of computing power each contributed. This collaboration makes mining more accessible to individuals who might not have the resources to mine alone, democratizing the process to some extent and ensuring that the network remains decentralized.

Impact on Network Security

Mining is not just about creating new coins; it's crucial for maintaining the security and integrity of the Bitcoin network. The process of cracking cryptographic puzzles to add new blocks acts as a deterrent against fraud and malicious attacks. Since altering any information on the blockchain would require redoing all the work of subsequent blocks, the computational effort (and thus the electricity and cost involved) needed to achieve such deceit is impractical. This built-in security mechanism is why Bitcoin remains remarkably secure despite its open and decentralized nature.

Evolution of Mining Technology

The technology behind Bitcoin mining has evolved significantly since Bitcoin's inception. Initially, miners used standard multi-core CPUs to mine Bitcoin. However, as the difficulty of the puzzles increased, the community discovered that graphics processing units (GPUs) were much more effective at solving Bitcoin's hashing puzzles. GPUs were followed by Field-Programmable Gate Arrays (FPGAs) and then Application-Specific Integrated Circuits (ASICs), each more powerful and energy-efficient than the last. ASICs are now the standard mining hardware for Bitcoin due to their ability to perform hash calculations at a much faster rate than CPUs or GPUs while also using less power. This evolution reflects the growing complexity and competitiveness of Bitcoin mining, but it also raises concerns about the increasing centralization of mining power in the hands of those who can afford these expensive technologies.

Reflection Section

As you delve deeper into the mechanics of Bitcoin mining, consider the balance between the democratizing potential of mining pools and the centralizing force of advanced mining technologies. Reflect on how these dynamics affect the overall security and distribution of power within the Bitcoin network. What are your thoughts on the sustainability of Bitcoin mining, considering the vast amount of energy it consumes? How do you see technological advancements shaping the future of mining?

Understanding the mining process provides a window into the technical wizardry that keeps Bitcoin secure and functional. As we explore further, the complexities of Bitcoin mining unfold, revealing not just a race for new coins but a robust mechanism that supports the entire Bitcoin ecosystem.

The Significance of Hash Rates in Mining

When stepping into the realm of Bitcoin mining, one term that frequently pops up is 'hash rate.' This might sound like something out of a complex math class, but it's actually a critical element in the mining process. Think of the hash rate as the horsepower of a car in the world of Bitcoin mining—it represents the mining power of the network. Specifically, hash rate refers to the number of calculations that a given network can perform each second. It's a vital metric that tells us about the health and the strength of the Bitcoin mining network. High hash rates mean more security and more efficiency, which are crucial in preventing attacks and processing transactions smoothly.

The relationship between the hash rate and mining difficulty is a dynamic interaction that ensures the stability of how new blocks are added to the blockchain. Mining difficulty adjusts approximately every two weeks or every 2016 blocks, which is designed to ensure that no matter how much mining power is added to the network, the average time to find a block remains about ten minutes. When more miners join the network and the hash rate increases, the puzzles become more difficult to solve. Conversely, if the hash rate drops, the puzzles become easier. This self-regulating mechanism maintains the pace of block creation, ensuring that despite fluctuations in miner participation, the blockchain's functionality and security remain intact.

Understanding the hash rate is not just about gauging the processing power. It also serves as a barometer for the security of the network. A higher hash rate means greater resistance to attacks, making it exponentially more difficult for any single entity to take control of the network or to alter the blockchain. This security is paramount, not just for the integrity of transactions but for the trust in the Bitcoin system as a whole. In essence, a robust hash rate protects the network from potential threats, including the notorious 51% attack, where an individual or group could potentially take control of the majority of the mining power and manipulate transaction confirmations.

The economic implications of hash rate fluctuations can be significant for miners. As the hash rate rises, the difficulty of mining also rises, requiring more computational power and, thus, more electricity. For miners, this means higher operational costs. When combined with the volatile price of Bitcoin, these factors can greatly influence profitability. Miners need to constantly assess the efficiency of their operations against the current hash rate and the price of Bitcoin. For instance, a sudden increase in hash rate without a corresponding rise in Bitcoin prices could reduce profit margins, pushing less efficient miners out of the market. Conversely, a decline in hash rate can lead to decreased difficulty levels, potentially making mining more profitable, especially if Bitcoin prices hold steady or increase.

Moreover, changes in the hash rate can affect transaction times and fees. During periods of low hash rates and network congestion, transactions can take longer to confirm, leading users to pay higher fees for quicker confirmations. This dynamic can influence user experience and the perception of Bitcoin's viability for daily transactions. On a broader scale, significant shifts in the hash rate could impact the entire Bitcoin market, influencing investor confidence and the cryptocurrency's price stability.

As you navigate through the complexities of Bitcoin mining, understanding the implications of hash rate is crucial. It not only affects your potential success as a miner but also impacts the broader Bitcoin network and market. By keeping a close eye on hash rate trends and adjusting your strategies accordingly, you can enhance your understanding and engagement with Bitcoin, making more informed decisions, whether you're mining, investing, or simply curious about how this groundbreaking technology operates.

Understanding Bitcoin's Algorithmic Framework

Peeling back the layers of Bitcoin's core, the SHA-256 algorithm emerges as a cornerstone of its cryptographic security. Developed by the National Security Agency (NSA) of the United States, SHA-256 stands for Secure Hash Algorithm 256-bit and is part of the SHA-2 family. It was selected for Bitcoin due to its solid security credentials and efficiency in processing. The primary role of SHA-256 in Bitcoin is to ensure that the data within the blockchain remains unaltered and secure. Every transaction and block in the Bitcoin network undergoes a SHA-256 transformation, which outputs a unique 256-bit signature for each. This signature acts as a digital fingerprint: unique, unrepeatable, and irreversible. If even a single character in a block is changed, the hash will change completely, signaling potential tampering to the network.

This hashing process is vital for maintaining the integrity and immutability of transactions. When a new block is created, its content is run through SHA-256, producing a hash that is then stored in the block header. This hash includes not only transactions but also the previous block's hash, creating a chain where each block is cryptographically linked to its predecessor. This linkage is what makes the blockchain immutable. To alter any information on a block, an attacker would need to recalibrate the hash not just for that block but for every subsequent block, a task that requires immense computational power and is, therefore, practically unfeasible. This cryptographic chaining defends the network against fraud and ensures that once a transaction is recorded in the blockchain, it is effectively impossible to alter.

Moving on to scalability, Bitcoin faces significant challenges as it grows. The SHA-256 algorithm is computationally intensive, and with the Bitcoin network limited to processing transactions in 1 MB blocks approximately every ten minutes, the system can handle only around 7 transactions per second (tps). In comparison, traditional systems like Visa can process thousands of tps. This limitation has led to bottlenecks and increased transaction fees, particularly during times of high demand. Several solutions have been proposed to address these issues. One notable attempt is the implementation of Segregated Witness (SegWit), which optimizes the space within each block by separating (or segregating) the transaction signatures (witnesses) from the transaction data. This segregation allows more transactions to fit within a block and improves the efficiency of transaction processing without altering the block size.

Looking forward, the Bitcoin community continues to explore potential adjustments to its algorithmic framework to better meet the evolving needs and challenges. One of the most significant concerns is quantum resistance. Quantum computing promises to bring vast improvements in processing power but also poses new risks to cryptographic systems like SHA-256. Although current quantum computers are not yet capable of breaking Bitcoin's cryptography, future advancements might make it possible. In response, there's ongoing research into post-quantum cryptographic algorithms that could potentially be integrated into Bitcoin's framework. These algorithms are designed to be secure against both classical and quantum computing threats, ensuring the long-term security of the network as computational technologies advance.

The continuous evolution of Bitcoin's algorithmic framework is a testament to the dynamic and innovative spirit of the Bitcoin community. As we navigate the complexities of cryptographic security, scalability challenges, and the looming advent of quantum computing, Bitcoin remains at the forefront of technological advancement in the cryptocurrency space. By understanding the underlying mechanisms that protect and power the network, we are able to appreciate not just the how of Bitcoin transactions but the why—why it remains secure, why it continues to attract attention, and why it stands as a pioneering force in the digital currency landscape.

Innovations in Bitcoin: Lightning Network and Beyond

When you think about using Bitcoin for everyday transactions— buying a cup of coffee, for example, the hesitation often comes from the wait times and fees associated with Bitcoin's blockchain. Enter the Lightning Network. This is a second-layer solution that operates on top of Bitcoin's existing blockchain, aiming to make transactions faster and more cost-effective. What this means for you is that Bitcoin can potentially handle transactions as quickly and inexpensively as swiping a credit card.

Introduction to the Lightning Network

The Lightning Network isn't just a minor tweak to how Bitcoin operates; it's an ambitious overhaul designed to combat the scalability issues that have been a significant concern for Bitcoin since its inception. By enabling a system where transactions don't need to be immediately broadcast to the blockchain, the Lightning Network dramatically reduces the load on the network. This is crucial because the current model, where every transaction is recorded on the blockchain, leads to congestion and increased transaction fees, which in turn make microtransactions or everyday purchases impractical with Bitcoin.

How the Lightning Network Works

Imagine you and a friend decide to set up a tab that allows you to make multiple transactions between each other throughout the day without settling up after every exchange. At the end of the day, only the net amount is settled. The Lightning Network works similarly but on a much larger scale. It allows two parties to open a payment channel between them that exists off the blockchain. Once this channel is open, they can exchange Bitcoin an unlimited number of times without committing these transactions to the Bitcoin blockchain right away. Only when the channel is closed will the final balances be broadcasted to the public blockchain. This method not only speeds up transactions but also significantly reduces transaction fees, as the need to record every transaction on the blockchain is eliminated.

The real magic happens when these channels interconnect with others, forming a network where you can send payments to someone even if you don't have a direct channel open with them. The network automatically finds the shortest route through other connected channels. This interconnected network of channels greatly enhances Bitcoin's usability, making it not only possible but efficient for small, routine transactions.

Impact on Bitcoin Usability

The potential of the Lightning Network to enhance Bitcoin's usability for everyday transactions is vast. By shifting the transaction load off the main blockchain, Bitcoin can scale up to potentially millions of transactions per second—comparable to major credit card networks. This scalability makes using Bitcoin for small purchases, like a coffee or a book, not only possible but practical. It also opens up new avenues for Bitcoin in micropayments, such as tipping content creators or paying for articles on a per-view basis, avenues that were previously unfeasible due to high transaction costs and slow processing times.

Other Emerging Innovations

While the Lightning Network is one of the most promising innovations for addressing Bitcoin's limitations, it's not the only one. Sidechains and state channels are also pivotal in pushing Bitcoin's functionality forward. Sidechains are separate blockchains that are attached to the main Bitcoin blockchain. They allow for experimentation with new features without impacting the main chain. This can include features like smart contracts or different consensus mechanisms that make transactions faster or more secure.

State channels, similar to the Lightning Network, take the concept further by allowing not just Bitcoin transactions but any state changes to be conducted off the main blockchain. This could include changes in smart contracts or other forms of digital agreements. These technologies collectively expand what's possible with Bitcoin, making it more versatile and adaptable to more wide-ranging uses beyond just a digital currency. By enhancing Bitcoin's functionality and addressing its limitations, these innovations not only improve its usability but also ensure its relevance in an increasingly competitive blockchain ecosystem.

Navigating through these advancements, it becomes evident that Bitcoin is much more than just digital gold; it's a growing, evolving technology that continuously adapts to meet the demands of its users. From making your daily coffee run smoother with the Lightning Network to exploring new digital agreements with state channels, the innovations surrounding Bitcoin are making it more accessible and functional for everyday use. As these technologies continue to evolve and integrate with the Bitcoin ecosystem, they pave the way for a future where Bitcoin's potential is fully unleashed, transforming not just how we view this cryptocurrency but also how we interact with the digital world at large.

Future Technologies Shaping Bitcoin

As we peer into the horizon of Bitcoin's technological evolution, several groundbreaking advancements in cryptography and hardware are ready to reshape its landscape. These developments not only promise enhanced security and efficiency but also allow for greater adoption and new functionalities. Among these, homomorphic encryption and zero-knowledge proofs stand out as frontrunners in the cryptographic arena, offering robust privacy enhancements that could revolutionize how transactions and data are managed in the Bitcoin network.

Homomorphic encryption is a form of cryptography that allows computations to be executed on encrypted data, returning encrypted results that, when decrypted, match the results of operations performed on the plaintext. This means that data can be processed without ever exposing it in its raw form, significantly enhancing data privacy and security. For Bitcoin, this could enable new forms of secure data processing and verification that won't compromise the privacy of transaction details. Imagine a scenario where you could verify the validity of a transaction or perform complex financial audits without ever revealing the underlying data—homomorphic encryption holds the key to this ability.

Zero-knowledge proofs present another fascinating area of cryptographic advancement. These are methods by which one party can prove to another that a given statement is true without conveying any additional information apart from the fact that the statement is indeed true. For Bitcoin, zero-knowledge proofs could greatly enhance transaction privacy by allowing users to verify transactions as valid without revealing anything about the transaction's inputs or outputs. This would be a momentous step forward in protecting financial privacy, enabling users to enjoy the benefits of public blockchain technology without exposing their financial activities.

Turning to blockchain interoperability, the seamless exchange of value and information across different blockchain systems is a pivotal development on the horizon. Interoperability can be thought of as the ability for different blockchain networks to communicate and transact without barriers, akin to how email systems work across different hosting platforms. For Bitcoin, enhancing interoperability means that it could more easily connect with other blockchains, opening a myriad of possibilities for cross-chain collaborations and functionalities. This could facilitate everything from multi-chain asset transfers to complex smart contracts that operate across different networks, broadening Bitcoin's utility and appeal.

Advancements in mining hardware also continue to shape Bitcoin's future. The next generation of mining hardware may focus on energy efficiency and accessibility, reducing the environmental impact of Bitcoin mining and making it more accessible to average users. This could involve the development of new types of mining chips that consume less power or the use of renewable energy sources to power mining operations. Such innovations would not only make Bitcoin mining more sustainable but also allow the mining process to be available to more people, ensuring that it remains in the hands of the many rather than the few.

Lastly, the potential impact of quantum computing looms large as a disruptive force in the realm of Bitcoin. A quantum computer, with its ability to solve complex mathematical problems at unprecedented speeds, could theoretically break Bitcoin's cryptographic security. However, the Bitcoin community is proactive, with ongoing research into quantum-resistant cryptographic methods that could safeguard Bitcoin against even the most advanced computational abilities. By staying ahead of these technological curves, Bitcoin is not just reacting to emerging threats but is preparing to thrive in the next wave of technological evolution.

As we wrap up this exploration of future technologies shaping Bitcoin, it's clear that the landscape of digital currencies is anything but static. From enhancing security and privacy with advanced cryptography to fostering seamless interactions across blockchain networks and pushing the frontiers of mining technology, Bitcoin continues to evolve. These advancements are not just technical upgrades; they are transformative shifts that could redefine the global financial landscape, making it more secure, efficient, and inclusive. As we turn the page to the next chapter, the ongoing innovation in Bitcoin technology promises to keep us on the edge of our seats, watching as the future of finance unfolds before our eyes.

Chapter 6

Legal and Regulatory Aspects

Imagine stepping into a vibrant market where every stall offers something different. Now, envision that each of these stalls represents a country with its own set of rules on what can be sold and how. This is quite similar to the diverse and colorful landscape of Bitcoin's legal and regulatory status across the globe. As you delve into the world of Bitcoin, understanding this complex tapestry of laws and regulations is crucial, not just to navigate safely but to maximize your opportunities and protect your investments.

Navigating Bitcoin's Legal Landscape

Legal Status of Bitcoin

The legal recognition of Bitcoin varies dramatically from one country to another, painting a global picture that can seem as varied as the weather. In some places, Bitcoin is embraced warmly, like in Japan, where it's recognized as a legal method of payment. Contrast this with countries like Algeria, where Bitcoin is banned outright. Then there are nations like the United States and Canada, where Bitcoin is not considered legal tender but is recognized as a commodity or taxable asset. This classification impacts everything from how Bitcoin is traded to how it's taxed, making an understanding of regional legal distinctions essential for anyone engaged in Bitcoin transactions.

Regulatory Bodies Involved

As Bitcoin does not respect national borders, various international regulatory bodies have stepped in to provide guidelines and oversight. In the United States, for example, the Securities and Exchange Commission (SEC) plays a pivotal role in regulating cryptocurrencies deemed as securities. Meanwhile, the Commodity Futures Trading Commission (CFTC) considers Bitcoin a commodity, influencing how it's traded. The UK's Financial Conduct Authority (FCA) oversees the trading of cryptocurrencies, ensuring fair practices and the protection of traders. Each of these bodies has a significant impact on the market dynamic and operational practices surrounding Bitcoin, shaping the environment in which you trade and invest.

Compliance Requirements

Diving deeper into the mechanics of regulatory compliance, two critical protocols come to the forefront: Anti-Money Laundering (AML) and Know Your Customer (KYC). These protocols are not just bureaucratic red tape; they are essential safeguards designed to avoid illegal actions such as money laundering and the financing of terrorism. Compliance with AML involves monitoring and reporting suspicious activities, while KYC focuses on verifying the identity of individuals to prevent fraud. For you, the investor or user, this means undergoing identity verification processes when signing up with exchanges or wallets, ensuring that your activities remain transparent and within the bounds of legal frameworks.

Legal Challenges and Litigations

The path of Bitcoin through the legal landscape hasn't been smooth. Various legal challenges and litigations have tested the resilience and adaptability of this digital currency. Notable among these is the SEC's lawsuit against Ripple Labs, alleging that its XRP tokens were sold as unregistered securities. Such cases not only affect the parties involved but also set precedents that shape future regulatory decisions and market practices. For you, keeping an eye on these developments is crucial, as they could influence market sentiment and regulatory trends, impacting your Bitcoin holdings and strategies.

Reflective Exercise: Understanding Your Legal Environment

To further solidify your understanding of Bitcoin's legal landscape, take a moment to reflect on the following:

- How does the legal status of Bitcoin in your country impact your ability to buy, sell, or use Bitcoin?

- Are you aware of the primary regulatory body overseeing cryptocurrencies in your region?

- Have you encountered any challenges with AML and KYC compliance in your Bitcoin transactions?

This exercise isn't just academic—it's a practical step towards becoming a savvy participant in the global Bitcoin market, equipped with the knowledge to navigate complex legal terrains confidently.

Global Regulations on Cryptocurrencies: An Overview

In the dynamic world of cryptocurrencies, the regulatory landscape is as varied as the technology itself, with different countries adopting distinct approaches based on their economic policies, culture, and understanding of digital currencies. Broadly speaking, these regulatory frameworks can be categorized into three types: permissive, contentious, and restrictive. Each of these regimes not only reflects the country's posture towards digital innovation and financial security but also significantly influences the adoption and development of cryptocurrencies like Bitcoin within their borders.

Starting with permissive jurisdictions, these are countries that have embraced the potential of cryptocurrencies by implementing friendly regulations that foster growth and innovation. A prime example is Japan, one of the first major economies to recognize Bitcoin as a legal payment method. This acknowledgment came in April 2017, when the Japanese government amended its Payment Services Act to bring cryptocurrency exchanges under regulatory scrutiny while ensuring they adhered to vigorous standards for security and compliance. This move was largely seen as a response to the infamous Mt. Gox incident, which highlighted the need for regulation to build trust and protect consumers. The result of this regulatory clarity has been overwhelmingly positive, leading to a surge in adoption both among consumers and businesses, with Japan often seen as a global leader in the cryptocurrency space.

In stark contrast are the contentious regimes, where the regulatory environment is mixed or uncertain, often with ongoing debates about how to approach cryptocurrencies. The United States is a quintessential example of this category. While not outright hostile, the U.S. presents a complex patchwork of regulations that vary by state and the nature of the cryptocurrency activity. For example, the Securities and Exchange Commission (SEC) is actively involved in determining whether certain cryptocurrencies qualify as securities, which would make them subject to stringent regulations. This ongoing uncertainty can stifle innovation and deter new participants due to fears of unexpected regulatory clampdowns. However, it also reflects a cautious approach aimed at balancing the potential risks and benefits of cryptocurrencies, protecting investors while trying not to hinder technological advancements.

On the more restrictive end of the spectrum are countries like China, which have taken a firm stance against the decentralized nature of cryptocurrencies and, in 2017, banned cryptocurrency exchanges and Initial Coin Offerings (ICOs) because of concern about the financial risks and potential for fraud associated with unregulated markets. More recently, in 2021, China extended this ban to include all cryptocurrency transactions and mining activities, quoting concerns over financial stability and environmental impact. This crackdown reflects China's broader strategy of controlling capital flows and maintaining the integrity of its financial system while also paving the way for the introduction of its digital currency, the Digital Yuan. The impact of these restrictive measures has been profound, leading to a significant drop in trading volumes within China and a migration of cryptocurrency businesses and miners to more crypto-friendly countries.

Amidst these diverse national approaches, international regulatory bodies, such as the Financial Action Task Force (FATF), perform a crucial role in shaping a cohesive global response to the challenges posed by cryptocurrencies. The FATF has developed guidelines that recommend measures for combating money laundering and terrorist financing associated with cryptocurrencies. These guidelines encourage countries to adopt regulatory practices that ensure that cryptocurrencies are not used for illicit activities while supporting innovation and financial inclusion. The FATF's efforts represent an attempt to bring a degree of harmonization to global cryptocurrency regulations, facilitating international cooperation and reducing the risk of regulatory arbitrage, where entities might move operations to jurisdictions with looser regulations.

Navigating this multifaceted regulatory landscape requires vigilance and adaptability. For you, as a participant in the cryptocurrency market, understanding the regulatory environment in each country where you operate is crucial. It not only helps you comply with the law but also helps you make informed decisions about where and how to conduct your cryptocurrency activities. Whether you're a casual investor, a serious trader, or a business leveraging cryptocurrency technology, staying informed about these regulations can help mitigate risks and capitalize on opportunities in the ever-evolving world of digital currencies.

Tax Implications for Bitcoin Investors

Navigating the tax implications of Bitcoin investments can seem like finding your way through a labyrinth, especially given the variations in tax treatment across different jurisdictions. When it comes to taxes, Bitcoin doesn't quite fit neatly into any traditional category—it's treated differently depending on where you are in the world. For example, in the United States, the Internal Revenue Service (IRS) classifies Bitcoin as property, not currency. This means that, much like owning real estate, any gain from the sale or exchange of Bitcoin is taxed as capital gains. This treatment aligns with how stocks and bonds are handled, where the purchase price (or basis) and the price at the time of sale determine the capital gain or loss reported on tax returns.

The specifics of reporting these transactions can be quite meticulous. In the U.S., every transaction involving Bitcoin, whether it's buying a cup of coffee or trading for another digital currency, must be reported on your tax returns. To do this effectively, maintaining thorough records of all your transactions is crucial—tracking the date of each transaction, the amount of Bitcoin involved, the value of Bitcoin at the time of the transaction, and the purpose of the transaction. This level of detail is necessary to accurately calculate any gains or losses, which are reported on Form 8949 and summarized on Schedule D of your tax return. The responsibility is on you to keep detailed records, as failing to report income, even unintentionally, can lead to penalties and interest.

For Bitcoin investors looking to optimize their tax situation, several strategies can be employed. Timing your disposals, for instance, can significantly impact your tax liability. In many places, the rate of tax you'll pay on capital gains can depend on how long you've held an asset. Typically, assets held for longer than a year may qualify for lower tax rates on gains in many jurisdictions. Another helpful strategy is tax-loss harvesting, where you sell Bitcoin at a loss to offset a capital gains tax liability. This can be especially helpful in a volatile market where values fluctuate widely. However, if you wish to claim the loss as a tax deduction, it's essential to be aware of the wash-sale rule, which prohibits the repurchase of the same or substantially identical asset within a 30-day period before or after it's sold at a loss.

Despite these strategies, one common pitfall that many Bitcoin investors fall into is failing to report their investments and transactions. Whether from misunderstanding the requirements or underestimating the implications of their activities, these oversights can lead to significant issues with tax authorities. In some cases, if the omission is found to be willful, it could even result in criminal charges. The key to avoiding such outcomes is straightforward:

ensure compliance by staying informed about the tax regulations that apply to your Bitcoin activities and keeping meticulous records of all transactions.

Understanding and navigating the tax implications of Bitcoin investing are critical components of managing your investments wisely. By staying informed about them in your jurisdiction, diligently reporting all transactions, and employing strategies to manage tax liabilities, you can help ensure that your Bitcoin journey is both profitable and compliant. This proactive approach not only helps in optimizing your returns but also in maintaining a good standing with tax authorities, safeguarding your financial future in the evolving world of digital currencies.

Keeping Up with Regulatory Changes in Bitcoin

In the ever-evolving landscape of Bitcoin, staying informed about regulatory changes is not just beneficial—it's essential. Think of it as keeping a weather eye on the horizon; knowing when a storm is brewing or when clear skies can significantly alter your course and decisions. For those invested in Bitcoin, whether you're dabbling in mining, trading, or using it as a payment method, understanding the regulatory environment is crucial. Reliable sources for tracking these changes include government websites like the U.S. Securities and Exchange Commission or the Financial Conduct Authority in the UK. These sites often provide direct insights into current regulations and any forthcoming changes. Additionally, industry news outlets such as CoinDesk or The Block are invaluable for their timely and detailed analyses of how regulatory shifts across the globe could impact Bitcoin.

Moreover, any regulatory changes can have a profound impact on Bitcoin's market dynamics and investment strategies. For instance, a new regulation that affects how Bitcoin is mined could change the entire economic model for miners, influencing everything from the price of Bitcoin to its environmental impact. Similarly, changes in how Bitcoin is classified by financial authorities (think property vs. currency vs. commodity) can affect everything from your tax obligations to how you can use Bitcoin in your business operations. By staying informed, you can anticipate these changes, adjust your strategies accordingly, and ensure that you remain compliant and your investments are secure.

Engagement with regulatory bodies is another crucial element often overlooked by casual participants in the Bitcoin ecosystem. It's easy to think of regulation as something that happens 'to' us, but in reality, it's a dialogue. Participating in this dialogue can help shape policies that are fair and knowledgeable of the benefits of Bitcoin. Many regulatory bodies are open to feedback and often hold consultations with stakeholders before finalizing regulations. Getting involved in these discussions, either directly or through industry associations, can help ensure that the regulatory environment evolves in a way that supports innovation while protecting users.

Lastly, preparing for compliance involves more than just passively watching the regulatory landscape; it requires active preparation and adaptation. This might mean consulting with legal experts who specialize in cryptocurrency to understand how new regulations affect your particular situation. It also means implementing systems and processes that allow you to remain flexible and responsive to change. For businesses, this could involve developing compliance protocols that are easy to update as regulations change. For individual investors, it might mean setting up alerts or dedicating time each week to review the latest regulatory news.

Navigating the regulatory changes in Bitcoin doesn't have to be a daunting task. By leveraging reliable sources for information, understanding the potential impacts of regulatory shifts, engaging with policymakers, and preparing for compliance, you can ensure that you not only stay within the legal boundaries but also use these regulations to your advantage. As we close this chapter, remember that the landscape of Bitcoin regulation is continuously shaping the future of cryptocurrency. By staying informed and engaged, you equip yourself with the knowledge and tools needed to navigate this dynamic terrain successfully. As we move forward, the insights gained here will be invaluable in exploring the security aspects of Bitcoin in the next chapter, ensuring that your journey in cryptocurrency is secure and compliant.

Chapter 7

Security and Safety in Bitcoin Investment

Best Practices for Bitcoin Security

Imagine you've just stepped into the role of a digital bank vault manager, where every decision you make directly influences the safety and security of not just your assets but also those of others who trust your judgment. This scenario isn't far from reality when you dive into the world of Bitcoin investment. Here, every security measure you implement acts as a robust line of defense against potential threats. Let's explore some essential practices that are akin to setting up advanced, multi-layered security protocols for your digital vault.

Multi-Factor Authentication (MFA)

One of the first and most crucial steps in fortifying your Bitcoin security is enabling Multi-Factor Authentication (MFA) on all cryptocurrency-related accounts. Think of MFA as a series of different locks on your vault, where a thief would need to bypass not just one but multiple security checks. Typically, MFA combines something you know (like a password), something you have (like a smartphone for receiving a verification code), and something you are (like your fingerprint). By activating MFA, you significantly reduce the risk of unauthorized access, even if one of your security factors is compromised. This added layer effectively blocks intruders at multiple checkpoints, ensuring that accessing your digital funds is no easy feat.

Cold Storage Solutions

As you probe deeper into Bitcoin security, you'll encounter the concept of 'cold storage'—an effective method to keep your digital currency offline and out of reach from online threats. Cold storage solutions, hardware wallets, for example, are physical devices that store your Bitcoins away from the internet. These devices can be as small as a USB stick but come fortified with highly sophisticated security measures designed to protect your private keys—the digital codes that permit you to spend your Bitcoins. Unlike 'hot wallets' (Bitcoin wallets connected to the internet), hardware wallets are immune to viruses and remote hacking attempts, making them one of the safest options for the long-term storage of substantial Bitcoin holdings. Think of these as high-security vaults buried in a mountain, accessible only to you and impervious to external threats.

Secure Internet Practices

Navigating the internet without adequate protection can be likened to walking blindfold through a minefield. When managing Bitcoin transactions, it's critical to adopt secure internet practices to safeguard your digital assets. This includes using Virtual Private Networks (VPNs) that encrypt your internet connection, hiding your data flow from prying eyes, and protecting your anonymity online. Additionally, steer clear of public Wi-Fi networks when conducting transactions or accessing your Bitcoin wallet. Public networks are often less secure and can be breeding grounds for cyber threats like 'man-in-the-middle' attacks, where attackers intercept data being transferred over the network. By sticking to private, secured networks, you ensure that your Bitcoin transactions remain confidential and protected from unauthorized interceptions.

Regular Software Updates

Keeping your software updated is akin to regularly renovating and reinforcing your digital vault's walls. Software updates often include patches for security vulnerabilities that could be exploited by hackers. This includes updating your Bitcoin wallet software, antivirus programs, and even the operating system of the devices you use for your Bitcoin transactions. Each update not only enhances features but also strengthens security, closing off chinks in your digital armor that could be exploited by new strains of malware or hacking tactics. In the fast-evolving world of technology, staying updated is staying protected.

Reflective Exercise: Check Your Security Setup

To further solidify your understanding and application of these security practices, take a moment to assess your current Bitcoin security setup:

- Have you enabled MFA on all your cryptocurrency accounts?

- Are you using a cold storage option for your significant Bitcoin holdings?

- Do you consistently use secure and private internet connections for your transactions?

- When was the last time you updated your software and security programs?

This exercise is crucial in identifying any potential vulnerabilities in your security setup and underscores the importance of proactive measures in safeguarding your investments. As you continue to navigate the complex world of Bitcoin, remember that the security of your digital assets is paramount, and maintaining rigorous security practices is not just recommended; it's essential.

Recognizing and Avoiding Cryptocurrency Scams

Venturing into the world of cryptocurrency can sometimes feel like navigating a bustling marketplace, where amid the legitimate vendors, there are also hawkers peddling counterfeit goods. The excitement and potential for profit can sometimes overshadow the need for caution, making it easy to fall prey to scams designed to exploit the unwary. In this landscape, being able to recognize common scams and understanding how to verify the legitimacy of cryptocurrency offers become essential skills for safeguarding your digital assets.

One widespread type of scam in the cryptocurrency space is the phishing attack, where scammers attempt to trick you into giving away sensitive information, such as your wallet's private keys or login details to your exchange account. These attacks often come in the form of an email or website that looks almost identical to a legitimate service you might use, complete with logos and branding. However, the devil is in the details—perhaps the email address is slightly off, or the website URL has a subtle misspelling. Falling for this scam can lead to unauthorized access of your cryptocurrency holdings, essentially handing over the keys of your digital vault to a thief.

Another common scheme is the fake Initial Coin Offering (ICO), where scammers create a convincing pitch about a new cryptocurrency or blockchain project. They'll set up sleek websites and populate them with complex whitepapers and impressive team bios, often stolen from legitimate projects or entirely fabricated. The allure here is the promise of getting in on the ground floor of a new coin that could potentially offer high returns. However, once they've collected enough investment from unsuspecting backers, these fraudulent operators vanish, leaving investors with worthless tokens.

Ponzi schemes are also rampant in the crypto world. These scams promise high returns on your investment through strategies that are vague or secretive, asserting that profits are generated through revolutionary trading or mining techniques. However, the returns are not actually derived from any legitimate business activities but rather from the funds contributed by new investors. Once the inflow of new investors dries up, the scheme collapses, with most participants losing their money.

To shield yourself from such deceptive practices, it's crucial to recognize the red flags. Promises of guaranteed returns should always raise eyebrows. The volatile nature of cryptocurrencies makes it impossible to guarantee profits, so such promises are practically a hallmark of a scam. Similarly, if details about the project are sketchy or unverifiable, or if you're pressured to invest quickly, it's wise to step back and reconsider. High-pressure tactics are designed to override your better judgment by creating a sense of urgency that isn't really there.

When considering an investment, always take the time to do your homework. Start by researching the developers behind the project. Are their identities transparent? Do they have a track record or digital footprint that can be verified? Critically reading the project's whitepaper is another essential step. Does it lay out a clear, feasible plan, or is it filled with buzzwords that sound impressive but offer little real substance? Also, look for endorsements from reputable sources within the cryptocurrency community. If respected figures or entities are willing to associate their names with the project, it adds a layer of credibility.

If you ever suspect that you've been targeted by a scam, taking swift action can help mitigate potential damages. This includes reporting the incident to the relevant authorities, such as the Internet Crime Complaint Center (IC3) or the Federal Trade Commission (FTC) in the United States. Additionally, alert the cryptocurrency exchange or wallet service you use, as they may be able to assist in securing your accounts or even recovering lost funds. While the recovery of lost funds isn't guaranteed, especially in cases involving cryptocurrencies, promptly reporting the scam can prevent further losses and help authorities crack down on scammers.

Navigating the cryptocurrency landscape requires both enthusiasm for new technology and a healthy dose of skepticism. By staying informed and vigilant, you can protect yourself from scams and focus on the genuine prospects that the world of digital currencies can offer. Remember, the most powerful tool at your disposal is knowledge, and taking the time to acquire and apply this knowledge is your best defense in the dynamic and often murky waters of cryptocurrency investment.

The Role of Encryption in Securing Bitcoin Transactions

Diving into the realm of Bitcoin, the backbone supporting its robust security framework is cryptography, a sophisticated method of protecting information by transforming it into a secure format. This process, known as encryption, is pivotal in safeguarding your Bitcoin transactions from prying eyes and ensuring they are not tampered with during transmission or storage. Let's break down these cryptographic techniques to understand how they create a fortress around your Bitcoin dealings.

Cryptography in Bitcoin utilizes a specific type of algorithm known as SHA-256, which is part of a larger family of cryptographic hash functions. Think of a hash function as a way of taking an input (or 'message') and returning a fixed-size string of bytes. The output, typically a 'digest,' is exclusive to each unique input, and it changes significantly even with a tiny alteration in input. This characteristic ensures that any attempt to alter transaction data in any way will result in a different hash value, signaling an alert to the network about potential tampering. These hash functions make the history of Bitcoin transactions immutable, meaning once a transaction is recorded on the blockchain, it cannot be changed without altering all subsequent blocks and achieving consensus from the network—a task so computationally intensive that it becomes unfeasible in practice.

Venturing further into the cryptographic landscape of Bitcoin, we encounter the critical role played by public and private key encryption. In this system, each Bitcoin wallet has a 'public key,' which you can think of as an address that others can see and send Bitcoin to, and a 'private key,' which is known only to the wallet's owner. The private key is used to digitally sign transactions, providing mathematical proof that the transaction has come from the owner of that wallet. This signature, which is sent to the network for verification, ensures that the transaction is secure and the sender is authenticated. The beauty of this system lies in its simplicity and effectiveness. While the public key is visible to everyone on the network, the private key remains confidential, ensuring that only the owner can initiate transactions from their wallet. Therefore, safeguarding your private keys is akin to holding the keys to your safe—losing them means losing access to your Bitcoin.

To enhance transaction security further, advanced practices such as the use of multi-signature addresses have been developed. These require multiple parties to sign a transaction before it can be executed. This method is particularly useful in scenarios where you need to ensure that multiple stakeholders have approved a transaction, which adds an extra layer of security by distributing the permission to transact. You should also perform regular security audits of wallet platforms to help identify and mitigate potential vulnerabilities, ensuring that the wallet's infrastructure remains secure against evolving threats. These audits, performed by cybersecurity experts, examine everything from the software code to the user interface, ensuring that the wallet adheres to best security practices and that any potential security loopholes are closed.

Looking ahead, the horizon of cryptographic technologies holds promising developments that could further bolster the security of Bitcoin transactions. One of the most anticipated advancements is the development of quantum-resistant algorithms. With the advent of quantum computing, traditional cryptographic techniques could potentially be broken, exposing Bitcoin transactions to new types of threats. However, the Bitcoin community and researchers are already working on developing new types of encryption that can withstand the power of quantum computing. These future-proof cryptographic approaches aim to ensure that Bitcoin remains secure, even as the underlying technologies evolve.

Understanding these cryptographic principles and practices not only equips you with the knowledge to secure your Bitcoin transactions but also deepens your appreciation of the ingenuity behind Bitcoin's security model. As you continue to explore Bitcoin and engage in transactions, remember that the power of cryptography is a central pillar upholding the security and integrity of this digital currency. By staying informed about these techniques and the latest developments in the field, you can navigate the Bitcoin landscape with confidence, assured in the security of your transactions.

Backup and Recovery Solutions for Bitcoin Investors

When you're investing in Bitcoin, think of your digital assets as precious heirlooms in a family safe. Just as you'd secure and backup important family documents, your Bitcoin also requires a robust protection strategy—a strategy that ensures your digital wealth is safely backed up and recoverable in any eventuality. Let's delve into why backups are the cornerstone of digital asset security and how you can effectively safeguard your Bitcoin investments.

Importance of Backup

Imagine waking up one day to find that your digital wallet, holding all your Bitcoin, has become inaccessible or, worse, compromised. Without a backup, this scenario could mean a total loss of all your digital assets. This is where the importance of having strong backup solutions cannot be overstressed. Backups serve as a fail-safe, a way to restore your Bitcoin wallet if your primary access is lost due to device failure, theft, or a cyber attack. By maintaining a current backup, you ensure that you retain access to your funds under any circumstances. The key here is redundancy; having multiple backups in diverse forms and locations enhances the security and accessibility of your assets.

Digital vs. Physical Backups

In the realm of Bitcoin, backups can generally be categorized into two types: digital and physical. Digital backups, such as those stored on USB drives or external hard drives, offer convenience and quick access. They can be encrypted and stored in multiple locations, such as safe deposit boxes or secure cloud storage services that allow for encrypted data uploads. However, be aware that digital backups also carry the risk of being corrupted by malware or targeted by cyberattacks if not properly secured.

On the other hand, physical backups, such as paper wallets or metallic backups (where recovery phrases are engraved on metal for durability), provide an entirely offline option that completely eliminates the risk of online threats. These backups, however, are susceptible to physical hazards like fire, water damage, or even being misplaced. For the utmost security, it's prudent to use a combination of both digital and physical backups, leveraging the strengths of each to safeguard your investment.

Secure Backup Practices

To ensure the effectiveness of your backups, follow these best practices: First, utilize encrypted storage media for digital backups. Encryption adds an additional layer of security, making it difficult for unauthorized users to access your data even if they physically possess your backup device. Second, diversify the locations of your backups. This could mean keeping a USB drive in a safe at home, another in a safe deposit box at a bank, and perhaps a third with a trusted family member in a different geographic location. This strategy protects against the loss of your Bitcoin due to local disasters or theft.

Additionally, consider the use of tamper-evident bags or safes for physical backups. These can provide visible evidence if someone has attempted to access them, adding an extra layer of security. Regularly update your backups, especially after every transaction or when changes are made to your wallet's security settings. This ensures that the backup is current and all recent transactions are preserved.

Recovery Process

If the need arises to recover your Bitcoin wallet using your backup, the process should be approached with caution to avoid compromising your security. Begin by ensuring that the device or system you are using for recovery is secure and free of malware. Install a fresh, trusted version of your wallet software and prepare to enter your recovery phrase. This phrase, usually consisting of 12 to 24 words, acts as the key to restoring your wallet and its contents.

During recovery, it's crucial to enter the recovery phrase exactly as it was generated. Any mistake in transcription can prevent access to your funds. Once the wallet is restored, immediately create a new backup of the recovery phrase and consider transferring your funds to a new wallet with a freshly generated private key and recovery phrase. This move is especially recommended if you suspect that your previous wallet might have been compromised in any way.

By adhering to these backup and recovery protocols, you can be sure that your Bitcoin investments remain secure and accessible, no matter what challenges you might face. Regularly revisiting and updating your backup strategy is also crucial, as it keeps you prepared and responsive to the ever-evolving landscape of digital security threats. Remember, in the world of Bitcoin, proactive measures are the best defense against potential losses.

The Future of Cryptocurrency Security

As we navigate the developing landscape of cryptocurrency, it's clear that the frontier of digital security is expanding rapidly, introducing innovative technologies and practices that promise to redefine how we protect our digital assets. Among these advancements, biometric security systems stand out as a particularly promising development. Biometric systems use unique physical characteristics, such as fingerprints, iris patterns, or even facial recognition, to authenticate identity. This method could significantly enhance the security of cryptocurrency wallets and transactions by ensuring that access is strictly tied to the verified user. Imagine a world where accessing your digital wallet is as simple and secure as looking into a device that scans your iris. This technology isn't just futuristic—it's becoming increasingly practical and is poised to set new standards in securing personal and financial data.

Another intriguing area of development is decentralized identity verification, which leverages blockchain technology to create a secure, immutable identity for each user. This method could revolutionize security by making it exceedingly difficult for anyone to steal your identity. In a decentralized system, your identity isn't stored in a central database that is vulnerable to breaches. Instead, it's spread across a blockchain, accessible only through complex cryptographic protocols. This approach not only enhances security but also preserves privacy, giving you control over who can access your personal information and how it's used.

As these technologies develop, we must also consider the impact of regulatory changes within the cryptocurrency industry. Regulatory bodies worldwide are beginning to recognize the need for updated standards and compliance requirements to address the unique challenges that are posed by digital currencies. These changes could introduce new security protocols, such as stricter verification processes or mandatory compliance checks, which could, in turn, foster a safer trading environment. However, these regulations will need to strike a balance between enhancing security and preserving the innovation and accessibility that make cryptocurrencies unique.

Moreover, the role of education and community engagement in improving security cannot be overstated. As the cryptocurrency landscape grows, so does the need for comprehensive education on safe investment and trading practices. Community-driven initiatives and educational programs can play a crucial role in raising awareness about security best practices and emerging threats. By fostering a well-informed community, we can create a collective defense against scams, hacks, and other security threats, making the cryptocurrency ecosystem safer for everyone.

Looking ahead, we must also prepare for new threats that could challenge the security of our digital assets. Advanced phishing attacks and AI-driven hacking attempts are on the rise, employing increasingly sophisticated techniques to access secure information. These threats require us to be proactive and vigilant, constantly updating our security practices and staying informed about the latest cybersecurity developments. Preparing for these threats means not only adopting the latest security technologies but also anticipating potential vulnerabilities and responding swiftly to threats as they arise.

As we close this chapter on security and safety in Bitcoin investment, it's clear that the future of cryptocurrency security is both promising and challenging. Emerging technologies like biometric security systems and decentralized identity verification offer exhilarating possibilities for enhancing security, while ongoing education and community engagement are vital for maintaining it. As we continue to navigate this dynamic field, staying informed and proactive in our security practices will be crucial for safeguarding our digital assets against evolving threats. Looking forward, the next chapter will explore the real-world applications of Bitcoin, showcasing how this revolutionary technology is being used across various sectors to create a more connected and efficient global economy.

Chapter 8

Real-World Bitcoin Use Cases

Imagine walking into your favorite coffee shop, where the aroma of freshly brewed coffee envelops you. As you get ready to pay, instead of pulling out cash or a card, you simply scan a QR code with your smartphone and pay with Bitcoin. This isn't a glimpse into a distant future; it's a reality today in many parts of the world. Bitcoin, often revered for its investment value, is increasingly becoming a part of everyday transactions, from buying coffee to paying for services. In this chapter, we'll explore how Bitcoin is weaving itself into the fabric of daily commerce across the globe, enhancing the convenience of transactions and fostering financial inclusion in underbanked communities.

Everyday Uses of Bitcoin Around the World

Bitcoin's journey from a niche digital asset to a widely accepted medium of exchange is nothing short of remarkable. Businesses and consumers worldwide are adopting Bitcoin, drawn by its benefits such as lower transaction fees and the ease of cross-border transactions. Unlike traditional banking transactions, which may be costly and slow, especially internationally, Bitcoin transactions can be completed swiftly and without hefty fees. This is because Bitcoin transactions bypass banks and directly connect buyers and sellers.

The adoption of Bitcoin by merchants and retailers is on the rise, driven by the desire to tap into a global customer base and reduce transaction costs. From small cafes and independent artisans to large online platforms, businesses are finding Bitcoin an attractive alternative to conventional payment methods. For instance, a boutique in Tokyo might accept Bitcoin to cater to tech-savvy tourists, while an online software vendor in the U.S. might do so to avoid the fees associated with credit card transactions. These businesses will not only enjoy reduced costs but also gain access to a broader, more diverse customer base that prefers using digital currencies.

Moreover, Bitcoin is making significant inroads in underbanked regions of the world, where traditional banking services are scarce or non-existent. In many parts of Africa and Southeast Asia, people are using Bitcoin to conduct transactions and store value. Unlike banks, Bitcoin does not require a physical presence or extensive documentation to access. Anyone with a smartphone and an internet connection can set up a Bitcoin wallet and start transacting. This accessibility is revolutionizing financial participation and empowerment in these regions, offering people more control over their financial lives.

However, the adoption of Bitcoin is not without challenges. Unpredictability in its value can make day-to-day transactions tricky. If the price of Bitcoin declines after being accepted as payment, a merchant might find themselves at a loss. Similarly, consumers might hesitate to spend Bitcoin if they expect its value to increase. To address these challenges, solutions like the Lightning Network are emerging. This technology enables faster and cheaper transactions on a separate layer of the Bitcoin blockchain, making it more practical for everyday transactions. By mitigating the issues of transaction speed and costs, technologies like the Lightning Network are making Bitcoin a more practical decision for everyday use.

As it continues to evolve, Bitcoin's role in daily transactions is only expected to grow. With advancements in technology and more stable regulatory environments, we might soon see a world where Bitcoin is as common in our daily lives as traditional money. Whether it's paying for a meal, sending money across borders, or accessing financial services, Bitcoin is set to transform how we think about and use money in our everyday lives.

Bitcoin in E-commerce: A Growing Trend

The digital marketplace is buzzing, not just with consumers clicking through an overabundance of products but also through the increasing incorporation of Bitcoin as a payment method. This trend is reshaping e-commerce, providing both businesses and consumers with advantages that stretch beyond conventional monetary transactions. For businesses, Bitcoin offers a reduction in chargeback fraud. Unlike credit card payments, Bitcoin transactions, once confirmed by the network, are irreversible, effectively quashing fraudulent claims of non-delivery or unsatisfactory service after the goods have been received. For consumers, the allure lies in enhanced privacy; Bitcoin purchases do not require the disclosure of personal financial information, which reduces the risk of identity theft, something all too common in online shopping environments.

Consider the case of Overstock.com, one of the first major online retailers to welcome Bitcoin back in 2014. This move not only widened their market reach but also decreased transaction costs compared to traditional credit card payments. The system they use, a Bitcoin payment gateway, seamlessly converts Bitcoin into the store's base currency at the point of sale, protecting them from price unpredictability. This setup exemplifies a successful integration of cryptocurrency into existing financial operations, offering insight into how other platforms might adopt similar strategies.

However, integrating Bitcoin into e-commerce is not without challenges. Price volatility remains a significant hurdle. The value of Bitcoin can dramatically fluctuate within short periods, potentially complicating pricing and profitability. To lessen this problem, many businesses convert Bitcoin payments into fiat currency immediately upon receipt, thus sidestepping any potential devaluation if the market takes a downturn. Regulatory uncertainty also poses a challenge, as the legal landscape for cryptocurrencies is still evolving. Companies venturing into Bitcoin must navigate these waters carefully, staying abreast of new regulations to ensure compliance and avoid potential legal consequences.

Looking ahead, the role of Bitcoin in e-commerce appears to be ready for substantial expansion. Trends indicate a growing consumer demand for alternative payment methods that offer enhanced security and privacy. Additionally, the rise of decentralized marketplaces, platforms that operate on blockchain technology enabling peer-to-peer transactions without the need for a central authority, could further accelerate the adoption of Bitcoin in online shopping. These marketplaces not only support the use of cryptocurrencies but also align with the decentralized ethos of Bitcoin, potentially creating new e-commerce ecosystems where Bitcoin is the preferred currency.

As these trends evolve, the landscape of e-commerce will likely continue to adapt, incorporating Bitcoin not as an alternative but as a mainstay payment method that offers distinct advantages over traditional fiat currencies. The continuing developments in blockchain technology and the increasing stabilization of Bitcoin's market will play crucial roles in shaping this future, potentially transforming how we think about buying and selling in the digital age.

Bitcoin and Remittances: Facilitating Global Money Transfers

In the bustling corridors of global migration, money flows steadily from economic migrants and expatriates sending earnings back home. Traditionally, this process has been dominated by wire services and banks, often chipping away a significant chunk of hard-earned money in fees. Enter Bitcoin, a beacon of efficiency, offering a faster and cheaper channel for these cross-border money transfers. The role of Bitcoin in remittances is increasingly pivotal, especially in its ability to reduce transaction costs dramatically and speed up the process, bypassing the cumbersome and expensive intermediaries typically involved in such transfers.

One of the most profound benefits Bitcoin offers is for migrant workers and their families. Consider the scenario where a worker in the United States sends money back to their family in the Philippines. Traditional methods can be costly and slow, with fees eating into the amount sent and delays in the funds becoming available. Bitcoin changes this equation. By using Bitcoin, the worker can send money instantly at a fraction of the cost, with the family receiving it directly into their digital wallet or converting it to local currency through a local Bitcoin exchange. This immediacy can be crucial during emergencies when families back home urgently need financial support. Furthermore, these lower fees mean more of the money earned makes its way to where it's desperately needed rather than being lost to transaction fees.

The impact of this shift is palpable in specific countries where remittances form a substantial part of the economy. In El Salvador, for instance, these payments account for about 20% of the GDP. The country's move to adopt Bitcoin as legal tender is partly aimed at making it easier and cheaper for its citizens working abroad to send money home. This has not only economic but also significant social implications, enhancing the well-being of communities by boosting their disposable income, which can be spent on education, healthcare, and investment in local businesses.

However, the path of Bitcoin in remittances isn't without its hurdles, as regulatory and practical challenges abound. Different countries have variable regulations regarding the use of cryptocurrencies, affecting how easily Bitcoin can be used. For instance, while some countries like El Salvador have embraced it, others have imposed strict regulations that can complicate the use of Bitcoin. Moreover, the issue of currency conversion remains a practical challenge. While receiving money in Bitcoin is efficient, converting it to local currency can still incur costs and requires a local exchange that accepts Bitcoin. This conversion can also introduce a layer of complexity in terms of fluctuating exchange rates, which can potentially affect the final amount received.

Navigating these challenges requires a nuanced approach. In regions where regulatory hurdles are significant, advocacy for more favorable policies could be necessary. Education also plays a crucial role—both senders and receivers must understand how Bitcoin works and the best practices for using it in remittances. As for the practical challenges, the development of more robust local exchanges and the wider acceptance of Bitcoin can help mitigate these issues, making the process smoother and more beneficial for all parties involved.

As we continue to explore the evolving role of Bitcoin in the global remittance market, it's clear that its potential to transform this vital financial flow is enormous. By reducing costs and transaction times, Bitcoin not only makes it easier for workers to support their families back home but also contributes to the broader economic development of entire communities. As more countries and companies explore and adopt these processes, the area of global remittances might be poised for a significant transformation fueled by the efficiency and inclusivity offered by Bitcoin.

Philanthropy in the Bitcoin Era

In the evolving environment of giving, the emergence of Bitcoin as a tool for philanthropy is reshaping how charities and non-profit organizations interact with donors, offering a new avenue for engagement and contribution. The integration of Bitcoin into philanthropic efforts isn't just about embracing digital innovation; it's about tapping into the myriad benefits that this cryptocurrency offers, such as enhanced transparency, traceability, and accessibility. These features are particularly appealing to a sector where donors demand accountability and visibility on how their contributions are being utilized.

Charities and non-profits worldwide are increasingly accepting Bitcoin donations, drawn by the cryptocurrency's ability to provide clear, traceable records of transactions. Every Bitcoin transaction is recorded on a blockchain, offering a public, immutable ledger that tracks the flow of funds from donors to the intended projects. This level of transparency is compelling for donors who want assurance that their contributions are reaching the intended destination and being used as promised. Also, the security features inherent in blockchain technology reduce the risk of fraud, ensuring that donations are not misappropriated, a concern that can often plague charitable organizations.

The broader impact of Bitcoin on philanthropic efforts is profound. Take, for instance, the Pineapple Fund, a philanthropic initiative by an anonymous donor who pledged to donate 5,057 Bitcoins (valued at $86 million at the time) to various charitable causes. This fund supported projects across multiple sectors, including healthcare, water sanitation, and human rights. The Pineapple Fund's approach not only demonstrated the substantial impact that Bitcoin can have on philanthropy but also set a precedent for other high-net-worth individuals in the crypto community to follow suit. By providing a high-profile example of how cryptocurrencies can be leveraged for social good, the fund has encouraged more organizations to adopt this technology.

Another significant aspect of Bitcoin in philanthropy is its impact on donor engagement. Cryptocurrencies are particularly popular among younger, tech-savvy generations who are comfortable with digital technologies and value the simplicity and efficiency that digital transactions offer. For charities looking to engage this demographic, accepting Bitcoin can be an effective strategy. It aligns with the preferences of younger donors and fits seamlessly into their digital lives, making it easier for them to support causes they care about. Moreover, the novelty of using cryptocurrencies for donations can also serve as a talking point to raise awareness among potential donors, driving further engagement and support.

However, navigating the use of Bitcoin in philanthropy is not devoid of challenges. The unpredictability of Bitcoin's value can complicate fundraising efforts, as the amount received by charities can significantly fluctuate depending on the market's state at the time of the donation. To manage this, some organizations immediately convert Bitcoin donations into fiat currency to lock in the value received. Additionally, regulatory scrutiny around cryptocurrencies can pose another hurdle. The legal landscape for Bitcoin is still evolving, and organizations must ensure they remain compliant with financial regulations, which can vary significantly by jurisdiction. This includes adhering to laws related to money laundering and reporting substantial cryptocurrency transactions.

Despite these challenges, the potential of Bitcoin to transform the philanthropic sector is undeniable. As more charities and non-profits become comfortable with blockchain technology and more donors look to cryptocurrencies as a viable means of contributing to causes, we could see a significant shift in how philanthropy is conducted. This shift not only promises to make charitable giving more transparent and efficient but also more inclusive, allowing people from all over the world to participate in philanthropy regardless of their access to traditional banking systems. As we continue to explore the juncture of technology and charitable giving, Bitcoin stands out as a powerful tool that could redefine the very nature of how we support and sustain social causes around the globe.

Innovative Bitcoin Projects Making a Difference

The innovative spirit of Bitcoin doesn't stop at financial transactions. It extends into decentralized applications (DApps) that are using Bitcoin's underlying blockchain technology to revolutionize other sectors. One of the most compelling applications is in identity verification. Imagine a world where your identity is completely secure and verifiable without the risk of fraud or theft. Blockchain technology offers this possibility by creating a decentralized database of identities that is almost impossible to hack because it is stored across a network of computers, not on a single server. This application is particularly crucial in areas where identity theft is widespread and can provide a secure way to verify individual identities in multiple settings, from voting to banking.

Furthermore, the transparency and immutability of blockchain are being harnessed in supply chain management. Companies like IBM are exploring how blockchain can track the journey of goods from manufacture to sale, ensuring that every step of the process is recorded and visible. This not only helps in verifying the authenticity of the products but also enhances the efficiency of supply chains by reducing the paperwork and improving the accuracy of tracking. For instance, a luxury item like a designer bag can be traced back to its origins, reassuring the customer of its authenticity and ethical manufacture.

Turning our attention to microfinance, Bitcoin is taking significant steps to provide financial services to small businesses in developing countries. These regions often suffer from a lack of access to traditional banking services, which can stifle economic growth and entrepreneurship. Bitcoin, through various microfinance platforms, offers a solution by enabling small loans to be distributed directly to businesses and entrepreneurs without the need for a banking intermediary. This process not only cuts down the cost of loans but also speeds up their disbursement, empowering small businesses to grow and scale quickly. The impact of such initiatives is profound as they enhance and encourage economic development and provide an opportunity to those who are often left out of the traditional financial system.

Mark Swanson

Environmental sustainability is another area where Bitcoin-related technologies are making a mark. Blockchain technology is being used to create clearer and more efficient systems for trading carbon credits, which allow businesses to trade emissions permits or credits on a secure platform, encouraging the reduction of carbon footprints in a verifiable way. Additionally, some projects are using blockchain to track the usage and trading of renewable energy. This not only helps in promoting the use of renewable sources but also ensures that the energy being consumed is indeed green and provides a reliable way to manage and certify green energy usage.

Looking to the future, there is a vast potential for Bitcoin and its associated technologies to impact various sectors of society. As global connectivity increases and technological advancements continue, we can expect to see an expansion in the scope and scale of these projects. The decentralized nature of blockchain, the security it offers, and its ability to create transparent, unalterable records suggest that its applications could extend far beyond what we currently envision. Whether it's to improve democratic processes, enhance data security, or promote environmental sustainability, Bitcoin's technology promises significant societal transformation.

In wrapping up this exploration of Bitcoin's innovative applications, it's clear that the implications of this technology extend far beyond simple monetary transactions. From revolutionizing identity verification and supply chain management to empowering small businesses through microfinance and promoting environmental sustainability, Bitcoin is proving to be a versatile tool that could reshape many aspects of our world. As we continue to discover and develop these applications, the potential for Bitcoin to drive meaningful change across various sectors appears both immense and promising.

Chapter 9

The Cultural and Social Impact of Bitcoin

Imagine you're exploring a new continent. The landscape is diverse, opportunities are abundant, and each step reveals more about this intriguing territory. This is much like delving into the cultural and social dimensions of Bitcoin. It's not just about the financial implications—Bitcoin is reshaping how we think about, interact with, and understand money and our economic systems.

Bitcoin's Influence on Financial Literacy and Responsibility

Enhancing Understanding of Financial Systems

Bitcoin isn't just a digital currency; it's a tour guide through the complex world of financial systems, monetary policies, and the importance of financial sovereignty. For many, Bitcoin is their first encounter with concepts such as inflation, the role of central banks, or how monetary policies affect everyday economic life. By its nature, Bitcoin invites you to question and explore these topics. It reveals processes that are often hidden or taken for granted within traditional financial systems. For instance, understanding Bitcoin leads to insights into what money really is—a form of consensus agreement, not just printed bills or numbers in a bank account.

Moreover, Bitcoin shines a light on the concept of financial sovereignty—the principle that individuals should have control over their own money without interference from governments or banks. This concept encourages you to think critically about your rights and responsibilities as part of the financial system. It challenges the existing state of affairs and provides a practical framework for understanding how money moves, who controls it, and how it can be managed in a decentralized environment.

Promoting Financial Responsibility

The decentralized nature of Bitcoin does more than reduce reliance on traditional financial institutions; it actively empowers users to manage their own finances. This shift in control can lead to a heightened sense of financial responsibility. By using Bitcoin, you're not just a passive participant in your financial life but rather an active director. Every transaction you make with Bitcoin requires a conscious decision, reinforced by the need to manage your own private keys securely.

This hands-on management can lead to a deeper understanding of financial risks and security. For instance, being responsible for your own Bitcoin wallet teaches you about the safeguards needed to protect digital assets. It's a practical lesson in risk management and security, providing real-world skills that are transferable to other areas of personal finance. Furthermore, the transparency of Bitcoin's blockchain allows you to meticulously track every transaction. This visibility promotes a mindset of accountability and vigilance, which are crucial components of fiscal responsibility.

Educational Resources and Communities

The rise of Bitcoin has spurred the growth of numerous educational resources, online courses, and community forums. These platforms help clarify Bitcoin's technology and implications, making it more accessible to a broader audience. For example, online forums and social media groups offer spaces where beginners can learn from more experienced users, ask questions, and share insights. Educational websites provide structured courses that cover everything from blockchain technology basics to advanced trading strategies.

This proliferation of learning resources has standardized knowledge about Bitcoin, allowing more people to make knowledgeable decisions about participating in this new financial landscape. It fosters a culture of continuous learning and engagement, which is essential in the rapidly evolving world of cryptocurrency.

Impact on Consumer Behavior

Bitcoin is also influencing consumer behavior, particularly in how people approach savings and investments. The finite nature of Bitcoin, with its capped supply of 21 million coins, highlights its potential as a long-term investment rather than just a medium for daily transactions. For many, investing in Bitcoin is a deliberate strategy for wealth accumulation, encouraging a long-term perspective on financial growth.

This shift is evident in how Bitcoin holders—often referred to as 'HODLers,' a term derived from a misspelled "hold" in an online forum—approach their investments. The term has come to define a strategy of holding onto Bitcoin long-term, regardless of unpredictability. This reflects a broader shift in consumer behavior towards saving and a more strategic approach to investment, influenced by the underlying principles of Bitcoin.

Reflective Exercise: Assessing Your Financial Literacy

To fully appreciate the impact of Bitcoin on financial literacy, consider how your understanding of financial systems has evolved since you first learned about Bitcoin. Reflect on the following questions:

- How has Bitcoin changed your views on money and monetary policy?

- What lessons have you learned about financial responsibility through managing Bitcoin?

- How have community resources and educational materials helped you navigate the complexities of Bitcoin?

Engaging with these questions can deepen your appreciation of how Bitcoin is more than just a financial asset—it's a tool for education and empowerment in the economic realm.

Bitcoin as a Tool for Financial Inclusion

In many parts of the world, traditional banking infrastructures are either absent or significantly underdeveloped. This lack of access locks out millions from basic financial services that many of us take for granted—like saving money securely or transferring funds. Bitcoin, however, is changing this narrative by providing a digital alternative that bypasses traditional barriers. With only a smartphone and internet access, individuals can engage in financial activities that were previously out of reach. This revolutionary aspect of Bitcoin is not just about technological advancement; it's about real human impact, offering new financial opportunities to unbanked and underbanked populations.

The transformative power of Bitcoin lies in its ability to provide access to financial services with unprecedented inclusiveness. Traditional financial systems often exclude individuals based on their credit history, earnings, or geographical location. However, Bitcoin operates on a different set of rules that don't discriminate. There are no credit checks, no need for a fixed address, and no hidden fees. Instead, the minimal transaction fees associated with Bitcoin and the absence of a need for a physical banking infrastructure make it an ideal solution for many in remote or impoverished areas. This accessibility is crucial in regions where the nearest bank branch might be prohibitively far away or in areas where political or economic instability makes traditional banking a risky affair.

Let's take a closer look at specific case studies that showcase Bitcoin's role in financial inclusion. In Venezuela, for instance, hyperinflation has rendered the local currency nearly worthless, devastating savings and making everyday transactions challenging. Here, Bitcoin has become not just a means of investment but a necessary tool for daily survival. Many Venezuelans are turning to Bitcoin to preserve their savings from inflation, pay for essential goods and services, and even receive payments from abroad. This shift to digital currency is a direct response to the inadequacies of the conventional financial system to provide stability and reliability.

Similarly, in Zimbabwe, where trust in the local financial system is low due to years of currency instability and hyperinflation, Bitcoin offers an alternative for preserving wealth. The ability to transact globally using Bitcoin has opened up opportunities for individuals and businesses alike, allowing them to bypass the local currency for more stable digital alternatives. It's a vivid demonstration of how Bitcoin can provide financial security in environments where traditional systems have failed.

However, the road to financial inclusion via Bitcoin is not without its obstacles. One of the primary challenges is the issue of technological literacy. Engaging effectively with Bitcoin requires a basic understanding of digital technologies, which can be a significant barrier in regions with low internet access and educational resources. Moreover, the volatility of Bitcoin can be a double-edged sword; while it offers opportunities for significant gains, it also poses risks of substantial losses, especially for those who might not be fully aware of or able to manage these risks effectively.

Regulatory hurdles also pose a significant challenge. In some countries, the legal status of Bitcoin is still unclear or subject to restrictive regulations that can hinder its adoption and use as a tool for financial inclusion. Navigating this complex regulatory landscape requires continuous monitoring and adaptation, which can be a daunting task for individuals and businesses alike.

Despite these challenges, the potential of Bitcoin to act as a tool for financial inclusion remains vast. Its ability to transcend geographical and political barriers presents a unique opportunity to redefine access to financial services worldwide. By continuing to address the challenges of technological literacy, volatility, and regulatory constraints, Bitcoin can significantly enhance its role as a liberating force for the financially oppressed, paving the way for a more inclusive global economy.

The Sociopolitical Implications of Bitcoin

Bitcoin's emergence as a digital currency has not only been a technological or financial phenomenon but a potent tool with profound sociopolitical implications. Consider this: in an era where political activism often meets with resistance or outright censorship, Bitcoin has emerged as a powerful ally for those looking to support causes without interference. The ability to make donations that bypass traditional financial systems and governmental oversight can be groundbreaking. This attribute of Bitcoin has been particularly valuable to activists and organizations operating in environments where dissent is suppressed, and financial transactions are heavily monitored. By using Bitcoin, they can receive funding from international supporters without alerting governing authorities, ensuring the continuity of their work in challenging political climates.

The impact of Bitcoin extends beyond just facilitating discreet financial support; it challenges the very fabric of national monetary policy and sovereignty. Traditional financial systems are tightly integrated with national governments, giving these bodies substantial control over economic policies and financial monitoring. Bitcoin disrupts this by providing an alternative that operates outside of these established systems. This decentralization not only reduces government control over financial transactions but also diminishes their ability to enforce economic sanctions or freeze assets. For countries whose economies are impaired by hyperinflation or fiscal mismanagement, Bitcoin offers their citizens an alternative to preserve and control their wealth independently, thereby challenging the state's monopoly over the economy.

In conflict zones or regions under oppressive regimes, Bitcoin's role becomes even more critical. For example, in countries where sanctions restrict the flow of currency, Bitcoin provides a lifeline by enabling transactions and remittances that would otherwise be impossible. This capability not only aids in humanitarian efforts but also supports small businesses and families that rely on international support to survive in war-torn regions. Bitcoin's decentralized nature ensures that it remains accessible even when traditional banking infrastructures are compromised during conflicts or governmental crackdowns.

However, the growing use of Bitcoin does not come without debate or legal considerations. One of the most contentious issues is its use for illegal activities. Due to its anonymity, Bitcoin has been criticized for facilitating illegal transactions on the dark web. This aspect has led to global debates about the need for regulation and monitoring of cryptocurrencies. While the anonymity of Bitcoin can be seen as a freedom-enhancing feature, it also poses significant challenges for law enforcement and regulatory bodies trying to curb illegal financial flows. The balance between preserving the privacy and freedom that Bitcoin offers and ensuring it does not become a tool for criminal activities is a delicate one, requiring subtle and thoughtful regulatory approaches.

These discussions are not just theoretical; they have real-world implications for the adoption and regulation of Bitcoin globally. As it continues to grow in popularity, its sociopolitical impact is likely to expand. Whether it's reshaping how activists fund their campaigns or challenging the control that governments exert over financial systems, Bitcoin is proving to be a significant force in the global socio-economic landscape. Its continued evolution will likely spark further debate and possibly reshape aspects of global finance and governance in ways we can only begin to imagine. As we navigate this evolving landscape, the dual promise and challenge of Bitcoin remain at the forefront, marking it as a pivotal element in the broader discourse on economic freedom and state sovereignty.

Bitcoin and Its Role in the Fight Against Economic Inequality

Wealth Distribution and Accessibility

The concept of wealth distribution often conjures images of immense disparities, where the scale of balance is tipped heavily in favor of those already at the top. Traditional financial systems are often criticized for reinforcing these inequalities, making wealth accumulation a challenging feat for the underprivileged. Enter Bitcoin, a tool that not only challenges these traditional systems but also offers a radical blueprint for redistributing wealth. Its accessibility to anyone with internet access democratizes financial opportunities, irrespective of geographic location or socio-economic status. This universal accessibility is pivotal; it means that anyone, from a farmer in rural Africa to a teenager in Southeast Asia, holds the same fundamental ability to access and utilize Bitcoin.

This level of accessibility is unprecedented in the history of finance. Traditionally, factors such as credit history, income level, and even geographical location could significantly influence your ability to access financial services. Bitcoin eliminates these barriers by offering a flat playing field where your value and ability to grow financially are not determined by your circumstances at birth. These implications are profound. By providing equal access to an appreciating asset, Bitcoin allows wealth to accumulate in corners of the world previously overlooked by traditional finance, potentially leading to a more impartial distribution of global wealth.

Empowering Marginalized Communities

By not only providing accessibility, Bitcoin has been a beacon of empowerment for marginalized communities. These are groups that have historically been excluded from the financial conversation—people who, due to various systemic and bureaucratic impediments, have found themselves on the periphery of economic activities. In regions where banking infrastructure is scant or non-existent, Bitcoin provides a viable alternative for financial engagement. For instance, small communities in remote areas can engage in Bitcoin mining or trading as a form of income and leverage cryptocurrency to build and sustain their local economies.

Furthermore, Bitcoin has enabled these communities to bypass corrupt or inefficient local banking systems. In countries where inflation rates are high and local currencies unstable, Bitcoin offers a more stable store of value, allowing individuals to preserve their wealth in a way that simply isn't feasible with their national currencies. The empowerment comes from having control over one's financial destiny. This control is not just about having access to financial products but also about having the right tools to positively influence one's economic conditions.

Bitcoin and Microeconomies

The impact of Bitcoin extends to the creation and sustainability of microeconomies, especially in developing regions. Here, Bitcoin is not just a digital currency but a catalyst for economic activity. Small-scale enterprises and individual entrepreneurs use Bitcoin to facilitate transactions that would otherwise be hindered by fiat currency limitations. For example, a local artisan in a developing country can sell their goods online and accept Bitcoin as payment, which can then be used to purchase raw materials, pay for services, or even invest in community projects.

These microeconomic activities foster a cycle of economic growth and reinvestment within the community. As more people adopt Bitcoin, the ecosystem grows, strengthening the local economy and providing a buffer against economic shocks from the national economy. This self-sustaining model illustrates Bitcoin's potential not only as a financial asset but also as a tool for economic development, providing a foundation upon which communities can build long-term economic stability.

Long-term Potential for Reducing Inequality

Looking to the future, the potential of Bitcoin to reduce global economic inequality holds promise but also warrants a nuanced exploration. As adoption spreads and access to technology increases, Bitcoin's potential as an equalizing force could see significant fruition, and we can envisage a world where access to Bitcoin mitigates the wealth gap currently worsened by unequal access to profitable investment opportunities. The decentralized nature of Bitcoin means that as it becomes more integrated into the global economy, it can play a pivotal role in leveling the financial playing field.

However, the path to this future is fraught with challenges. Technological advancements are needed to make Bitcoin more accessible and user-friendly for those not traditionally tech-savvy. Education also plays a crucial role; understanding Bitcoin and its implications requires a level of financial literacy that isn't universally available. Addressing these challenges is crucial for Bitcoin to fulfill its potential as a tool for reducing economic inequality. As we continue to navigate these waters, the evolving role of Bitcoin in the global economy remains a compelling narrative in the quest for financial equity and empowerment.

Bitcoin's Impact on Traditional Financial Systems

Imagine walking into your local bank, where transactions, approvals, and services all hinge on a centralized authority — a norm that has been unquestioned for decades. Now, enter Bitcoin, the proverbial new kid on the block, offering a decentralized alternative that is quietly revolutionizing the banking and finance sectors. This isn't just a minor disruption; it's a seismic shift in how financial transactions can be conducted. Bitcoin operates on a peer-to-peer network supported by blockchain technology, which ensures transparency and security without the need for a central governing body. This paradigm shift challenges traditional banking by providing faster transaction processing times, reduced fees, and enhanced accessibility, making it an attractive alternative for consumers and businesses alike.

As Bitcoin continues to carve out its niche, traditional financial institutions are not standing idly by. Originally met with skepticism, many banks and financial companies are now actively exploring the possibilities within blockchain technology. Recognizing the potential for improved efficiency and security, some institutions have started adopting blockchain to modernize their core operations and enhance customer experiences. Others have gone a step further by introducing their own digital currencies or offering cryptocurrency-related services. These moves are strategic; they not only allow these institutions to stay relevant but also enable them to tap into the new and rapidly growing market of crypto-savvy consumers.

Additionally, Bitcoin is reshaping investment strategies and portfolios across the globe, as what was once viewed as a fringe asset is now being taken seriously by individual investors and large financial entities alike. With its potential for high returns, even though accompanied by high volatility, Bitcoin is increasingly seen as a legitimate asset class. Investment funds specializing in cryptocurrencies are becoming more common, and traditional investors are diversifying their portfolios to include digital currencies. This shift is not just about capitalizing on financial gains but also about hedging against potential risks associated with traditional financial systems, such as inflation or geopolitical instabilities.

Exploring potential future scenarios for the coexistence of Bitcoin and traditional financial systems reveals a range of possibilities influenced by regulatory developments, technological advancements, and market integration. One scenario could see Bitcoin becoming a mainstream financial asset, integrating seamlessly into existing financial infrastructures. Banks might act as safe-keepers of digital assets, and Bitcoin could be used for daily transactions as well as long-term investments. Alternatively, if regulatory challenges become too great or if the volatility of Bitcoin remains high, it might remain a niche asset favored by a smaller group of enthusiasts and investors.

As we reflect on these developments, it's clear that Bitcoin is not just a passing trend but a significant player in the evolution of financial systems. Its continued impact on traditional banking, reactions from financial institutions, and shifts in investment strategies underscore a broader movement towards a more decentralized and digital financial landscape. This evolution isn't just about technology; it's about reimagining and reshaping the financial norms that have been in place for centuries.

As we close this chapter on Bitcoin's impact on traditional financial systems, we uncover how deep the roots of this digital currency are growing into the very foundation of financial practices. From disrupting the way banks operate to altering investment paradigms, Bitcoin is undeniably carving its path forward. As we step into the next chapter, we'll explore the technological underpinnings that make Bitcoin a unique and powerful player in the financial world, setting the stage for a deeper understanding of its mechanisms and potential.

Chapter 10

Looking Ahead: The Future of Bitcoin

Imagine the world of finance as a vast ocean, where traditional banking systems have long sailed as the predominant ships, guiding economic trade and monetary control. Now, picture Bitcoin and other cryptocurrencies as innovative, swift boats, zipping around and between these giant ships, empowered by the winds of technology and change. This chapter is about charting the course of these nimble crafts, exploring how they're not only navigating the waters but actively changing the tide of how financial transactions are conducted globally.

Emerging Trends in Bitcoin and Cryptocurrency

Integration with Financial Technologies

The integration of Bitcoin with developing financial technologies, particularly neobanks and fintech platforms, is akin to adding turbo engines to traditional banking vehicles. Neobanks, operating solely online without physical branches, embodies the synergy between digital banking and cryptocurrencies. They offer streamlined, user-friendly interfaces and cost-effective services, making them attractive to tech-savvy consumers who value convenience and efficiency. By integrating Bitcoin, these platforms not only expand their service offerings but also embrace the ethos of decentralized financial control and reduced reliance on traditional financial infrastructures. This fusion represents a significant shift in how you, as a consumer, can manage your finances—transcending international borders and accessing a global economic network at your fingertips.

Moreover, fintech platforms that incorporate Bitcoin are pushing the envelope in terms of offering innovative services like instant cross-border payments, micro-loans, and peer-to-peer transactions with reduced fees. These platforms are not only adopting Bitcoin for its novelty; they are harnessing its underlying blockchain technology to enhance security, increase transparency, and improve the efficiency of their operations. This trend is setting a new standard in the financial sector, prompting traditional banks to rethink their strategies and potentially adopt similar technologies to stay competitive.

Advancements in Scalability Solutions

Scalability is one of the most significant challenges Bitcoin faces, particularly the speed and cost of transactions. As Bitcoin continues to grow in popularity, the need for it to handle a larger volume of transactions is imperative. Currently, solutions like the Lightning Network, which operates as a second layer over the Bitcoin blockchain, are instrumental in addressing these issues. The Lightning Network allows for quicker and more cost-efficient transactions by enabling off-chain transactions, which are settled on the blockchain once the user decides to close out the channel. This method significantly reduces the burden on the main blockchain, allowing for increased transaction throughput.

Looking ahead, further advancements are expected in scalability solutions. Globally, developers and engineers are working on various upgrades and third-party solutions that promise to enhance

Bitcoin's ability to handle a growing volume of transactions while maintaining security and decentralization. These advancements are crucial for Bitcoin's adoption as a mainstream form of currency and can potentially revolutionize other areas of finance, such as real-time, large-scale transaction processing and microtransactions in internet-of-things applications.

The Role of Artificial Intelligence

Artificial Intelligence (AI) is set to play a transformative role in the evolution of Bitcoin and cryptocurrency. AI algorithms can analyze vast amounts of data from Bitcoin transactions to detect patterns, predict market trends, and identify potential security threats. This capability is incredibly beneficial for both individual investors and institutional players, as it can lead to more informed decision-making and enhanced risk management.

Besides, AI can automate complex processes such as compliance checks, wallet management, and customer support, making cryptocurrency platforms more user-friendly and efficient. As AI technology advances, its integration with Bitcoin could lead to more adaptive, intelligent, and responsive financial services, where transactions are not only secure and fast but also vigorously optimized for market conditions.

Influence of Institutional Adoption

The increasing interest in and adoption of Bitcoin by institutional investors and large corporations marks a significant milestone in its journey toward mainstream acceptance. This trend is indicative of Bitcoin's maturing market and perceived potential as a stable investment asset. Institutional involvement brings considerable market liquidity and stability, which can lead to more regulated and structured cryptocurrency markets.

As institutions integrate Bitcoin into their financial strategies, we can expect an increase in innovative financial products related to cryptocurrencies, such as Bitcoin futures, options, and ETFs, providing both retail and institutional investors with various investment opportunities. The influence of institutional adoption extends beyond investment portfolios; it validates Bitcoin's legitimacy as a financial asset and paves the way for broader market acceptance and integration into the global economic system.

As we steer through these emerging trends, the interplay between Bitcoin and advancing technologies paints a promising horizon, along with its integration into the broader financial ecosystem. The journey of Bitcoin is far from over; it's evolving, growing, and continuously reshaping the landscape of finance. As you navigate your own financial journey, staying informed and adaptable to these changes can not only enhance your understanding of Bitcoin but also empower you to make more strategic investment decisions in this dynamic digital age.

The Sustainability of Bitcoin Mining

When it comes to Bitcoin mining, the imagery that often springs to mind might be rows of machines whirring away, consuming vast amounts of electrical power. This scene has raised significant environmental concerns, given the substantial energy required to maintain the Bitcoin network. However, it's not just about energy consumption; it's also about the innovations and community actions aimed at steering Bitcoin mining towards a more sustainable future.

Let's delve into how the evolving landscape of Bitcoin mining is addressing its environmental impact and the role that regulatory and technological advancements are playing in this change.

The environmental impact of Bitcoin mining has been a hot topic, sparking debates and urging miners and the broader community to consider greener practices. One of the most promising developments in this area is the increasing adoption of renewable energy sources in mining operations. Solar, wind, and hydroelectric power are becoming more widespread as energy sources for mining farms, particularly in regions where these resources are abundant and cheap. This shift not only helps reduce the carbon footprint associated with Bitcoin mining but also improves the overall sustainability of the mining operations. Additionally, initiatives like carbon offset programs are gaining traction. These programs allow mining companies to invest in environmental projects to compensate for their carbon emissions, creating a balance that could lead to a reduction in the overall environmental impact of the cryptocurrency mining industry.

Let's consider the regulatory landscape, which significantly influences mining practices globally. As countries become more conscious of the environmental impacts of digital currencies, regulatory bodies are stepping in to set guidelines that encourage or mandate the use of renewable energy. For instance, some regions are exploring the implementation of policies that require cryptocurrency miners to use a certain percentage of renewable energy in their operations. These regulations not only promote a shift towards sustainability but also push the industry to innovate and find new solutions in order to meet these requirements. Furthermore, the scrutiny from regulators often leads to better reporting and transparency in energy usage, which can drive a broader shift across the industry towards more sustainable practices.

Technological advancements in mining hardware are also pivotal in enhancing energy efficiency. The development of more power-efficient ASIC miners is on the rise, with manufacturers competing to create hardware that offers more hashing power with less electrical consumption. The evolution of these devices means that the same amount of cryptographic puzzles can be solved using significantly less power, reducing the overall energy requirements of the mining process. This is crucial, as improved efficiency can drastically decrease the environmental impact per transaction, making Bitcoin mining more sustainable as the network scales.

Finally, the role of community-driven initiatives cannot be understated. Across the Bitcoin network, communities are developing numerous projects and protocols to promote sustainable mining practices. These include decentralized applications that allow for transparent tracking of energy consumption and the sourcing of green energy. Furthermore, mining pools focused on renewable energy are forming, providing a platform for miners who want to reduce their environmental impact by collaborating and sharing resources. These community efforts are instrumental in pushing the envelope regarding the possibilities of making Bitcoin mining an environmentally responsible activity.

As we explore these developments, it becomes clear that the narrative around Bitcoin mining is complex and evolving. The industry is at a crossroad where environmental sustainability is becoming just as important as profitability. With the collective efforts of miners, regulators, technologists, and the global community, the future of

Bitcoin mining looks not only greener but also more sustainable and efficient. This shift is crucial, not just in regard to reducing the environmental impact but also to ensure the long-term viability of Bitcoin as a leading digital currency.

Predicting the Long-term Value of Bitcoin

Predicting the future value of Bitcoin is a bit like forecasting the weather in an unfamiliar climate. There are observable patterns and a wealth of data, but the occasional storm can come out of nowhere, drastically altering the landscape. Over the long term, several factors are likely to influence Bitcoin's value: technological advancements, regulatory changes, market adoption, and macroeconomic factors. These elements intertwine in complex ways, making the cryptocurrency's future both fascinating and unpredictable.

Technological advancements play a pivotal role, particularly as Bitcoin continues to evolve. Innovations that enhance the scalability, security, and usability of Bitcoin will likely push its value upward. For instance, improvements in blockchain technology that allow for faster processing and verification of transactions can make Bitcoin more attractive to both consumers and businesses, increasing its utility as a medium of exchange. While advancements in cryptographic security might make Bitcoin even more secure, it's an essential factor when considering the increasing sophistication of cyber threats. As these technologies mature, they enhance the intrinsic value of Bitcoin, making it a more reliable and robust asset.

Regulatory changes are also significant influencers. As governments around the world better understand cryptocurrency, their approach to regulation will likely evolve. Positive regulatory frameworks can increase investor confidence and broaden Bitcoin's appeal to a broader audience, including institutional investors. On the other hand, stringent regulations may impose operational challenges, potentially stifling growth and innovation within the cryptocurrency space. However, it's also possible that hardship from tight regulations could foster innovative solutions that might circumvent or mitigate these challenges, thereby strengthening the ecosystem.

Market adoption encompasses everything from the acceptance of Bitcoin by merchants and consumers for daily transactions to its use by corporations and governments as a reserve asset. Widespread adoption hinges on Bitcoin's volatility, transaction fees, and ease of use, all of which are areas expected to improve with technological advancements and regulatory clarity. If Bitcoin were to become a standard for daily transactions or a reserve currency, this would significantly enhance its value, providing a stable demand base that could lead to price stabilization and increased valuation.

However, we cannot overlook the influence of macroeconomic factors, such as inflation rates, currency devaluation, and economic recessions. In environments where traditional fiat currencies are unstable, Bitcoin may be seen as a safer asset to store value, similar to gold. This perspective was particularly evident during high inflation periods in countries like Venezuela and Zimbabwe, where Bitcoin adoption saw substantial increases. If global economies face recession or significant financial crises, Bitcoin could similarly gain traction as a hedge against economic uncertainty.

Incorporating insights from financial analysts, economists, and blockchain experts provides a broader perspective on Bitcoin's potential financial trajectories. Many experts believe that as long as the fundamental aspects of Bitcoin, such as its decentralized nature, fixed supply, and increasing demand, continue to be relevant, it will maintain a significant value. Others caution about the speculative nature of cryptocurrencies and suggest a more conservative approach. These expert analyses are crucial as they provide grounded perspectives that balance the often polarized views found in general discourse.

As we consider the various scenarios of Bitcoin adoption—ranging from its use in daily transactions to becoming a reserve currency—the potential impacts on its value are profound. In a world where Bitcoin achieves widespread transactional use, we might see it becoming more stable, akin to traditional fiat currencies, but with an advantage due to its lower transaction costs and borderless nature. On the other hand, if Bitcoin were to be adopted as a reserve currency by even a small number of countries, the increase in demand and the consequential reduction in supply could drive its value significantly higher.

Each scenario presents a fascinating glimpse into the potential future of Bitcoin, colored by technological, regulatory, and economic factors. As you navigate the landscape of cryptocurrency investment, keeping an eye on these indicators can provide valuable insights into how Bitcoin might evolve and what that could mean for its value. Whether you're considering investing in Bitcoin or are simply curious about its prospects, understanding these dynamics is essential for anyone looking to grasp the potential of this groundbreaking digital asset.

How Bitcoin Could Shape the Future of Global Economies

Imagine a bustling digital marketplace where Bitcoin is not just a currency but a foundational element that influences how transactions are conducted, identities are verified, and businesses operate across borders. In this evolving digital economy, Bitcoin's role extends beyond a mere tool for financial transactions; it becomes a catalyst for redefining interactions in the online world. The integration of Bitcoin into digital identities is a significant advancement, providing a more protected and immutable method of handling identity verification processes. This could drastically reduce the instances of identity theft and fraud, making online spaces safer for users and businesses alike.

Likewise, Bitcoin's influence on online marketplaces could revolutionize e-commerce. By facilitating direct, peer-to-peer transactions without the need for intermediaries, Bitcoin could lower transaction fees, increase transaction speed, and open up global markets to sellers and buyers who previously had limited access due to financial barriers or restrictive banking regulations. This level of economic democratization could significantly alter the landscape of global trade, making it more inclusive and accessible to many. Additionally, Bitcoin's ability to effortlessly execute cross-border transactions at lower costs could transform international trade, allowing businesses and entrepreneurs in less developed economies to participate more fully in the global market.

The challenges Bitcoin poses to the traditional financial system are profound. By offering an alternate to government-issued currencies, Bitcoin questions the monopoly of national central banks on money supply and control. This could lead to shifts in global financial power dynamics, particularly if countries with unstable currencies see their citizens switch to Bitcoin or other cryptocurrencies. Such a shift could weaken the control those governments have over their national economies and spur changes in how global financial policies are crafted.

Bitcoin's potential to globally democratize economic participation is one of its most compelling aspects. By providing equal access to financial tools and resources, Bitcoin can level the playing field for people in different regions and socioeconomic backgrounds. Where access to traditional banking is limited or non-existent, Bitcoin can offer a viable alternative for storing value, making transactions, and even accessing credit. This could lead to increased economic activity and entrepreneurship, particularly in developing countries where a significant portion of the population is without access to banks.

The long-term socioeconomic impacts of Bitcoin could be transformative if its adoption continues to grow. Changes in the distribution of wealth are likely as Bitcoin and other cryptocurrencies provide new opportunities for wealth accumulation outside of traditional financial systems, which have often been criticized for favoring the already wealthy. Economic policies might need to be reevaluated and adapted to accommodate the rise of digital currencies, which do not respect national boundaries and are not easily controlled by any single entity. International trade practices may also evolve as cryptocurrencies like Bitcoin make it easier and cheaper to conduct transactions across borders. This could lead to a more interconnected and interdependent global economy where the traditional barriers of currency exchange and trade regulations are less significant.

As we look to the future, the potential of Bitcoin to reshape global economies is both exciting and challenging. Its role in the digital economy, its challenge to traditional financial systems, its potential for democratizing economic participation, and its long-term socioeconomic impacts are all areas that warrant close attention. Understanding these dynamics is crucial for anyone interested in the future of finance, technology, and global economic policy.

As this chapter closes, we reflect on the transformative potential of Bitcoin and its possible impacts on our global economic systems. The discussions here lead us to the broader consideration of digital currency's role in future societal structures, which will be explored further in the coming chapters. With each step forward, we inch closer to understanding the profound changes that Bitcoin could bring to our world.

Conclusion

As we wrap up our journey through the fascinating world of Bitcoin, from its humble beginnings amidst the 2008 financial crisis to its current stature as a pivotal force in global finance, it's clear that Bitcoin is more than just a digital currency. It has emerged as a formidable challenge to traditional financial systems. It is a tool for enhancing financial inclusion, as well as a catalyst for expanding financial literacy across the globe.

Bitcoin was created not just as an alternative investment asset but as a means to empower individuals with the independence to manage their financial resources without reliance on centralized institutions. Its potential to democratize access to financial services worldwide is one of its most compelling attributes, offering a beacon of hope for millions who are currently underserved by conventional banking systems.

Throughout this book, we've explored how Bitcoin is transforming financial literacy, with its underlying technologies making it more accessible and secure for users around the world. We've delved into the significant role Bitcoin plays in the economy and touched upon the environmental impacts of Bitcoin mining, acknowledging the community's ongoing efforts to address these challenges.

Here are the key takeaways: Bitcoin is not just a form of money or an investment but a movement towards a more equitable financial system. The importance of maintaining robust security in your Bitcoin investments cannot be overstated, and the need for continual education in this rapidly evolving sector is crucial.

I urge you to not just be a bystander but to actively engage in the Bitcoin ecosystem. Start small by investing a manageable amount, participate in online communities, and advocate for Bitcoin's adoption within your networks. Your involvement not only enriches your understanding but also contributes to the broader acceptance and success of Bitcoin.

The dynamic nature of Bitcoin and cryptocurrency means that staying informed is crucial. Keep abreast of developments by following reputable news sources, participating in forums, and utilizing a variety of educational materials. This ongoing learning process will help you navigate the complexities of the cryptocurrency world more effectively.

Reflect on how Bitcoin can influence broader socioeconomic issues and consider how you can be part of this transformative wave. Every individual action, whether it's using Bitcoin for transactions, investing, or simply educating others, plays a role in shaping our financial future.

Thank you sincerely for joining me on this enlightening exploration of Bitcoin. Your engagement and willingness to learn about this groundbreaking technology are what drive its ongoing evolution and success. I invite you to share your thoughts, experiences, and insights as you venture further into the world of Bitcoin investing and utilization.

Looking ahead, the future of Bitcoin is ripe with possibilities. While uncertainties remain, the potential for Bitcoin to forge a more inclusive, efficient, and transparent financial landscape is a vision that holds remarkable promise. Let's continue to watch, participate, and influence this exciting financial revolution.

Here's to taking control of our financial destinies and being part of a future where finance is genuinely global, decentralized, and accessible to all.

References

- *The 2008 global meltdown and the birth of Bitcoin - Mint* https://www.livemint.com/ Money/YTYMYUD7dytGK5PGSpdRTN/The-2008-global-meltdown-and-the-birth-of-Bitcoin.html

- *Blockchain: What It Is, How It Works, Why It Matters* https://builtin.com/blockchain

- *What Is Bitcoin Mining?* https://www.investopedia.com/terms/b/bitcoin-mining.asp

- *Cryptocurrency vs. Traditional Banking: Understanding the Differences and Benefits* https://www.globaltrademag.com/cryptocurrency-vs-traditional-banking-understanding-the-differences-and-benefits/

- *The History of Money: Bartering to Banknotes to Bitcoin* https://www.investopedia. com/articles/07/roots_of_money.asp

- *Decentralized Finance Will Change Your Understanding Of ...* https://www.forbes. com/sites/philippsandner/2021/02/22/decentralized-finance-will-change-your-understanding-of-financial-systems/

- *Venezuela's Bitcoin Story Puts It in a Category of One* https://www.coindesk.com/ business/2020/11/11/venezuelas-bitcoin-story-puts-it-in-a-category-of-one/

- *How Banks Are Adapting to Cryptocurrency* https://alphapoint.com/blog/banks-and-cryptocurrency/

- *How to choose the best Bitcoin wallet | Get Started with ...* https://www.bitcoin.com/ get-started/how-to-choose-the-right-bitcoin-wallet/

- *How To Buy Bitcoin - Investopedia* https://www.investopedia.com/articles/ investing/082914/basics-buying-and-investing-bitcoin.asp

- *What To Know About Cryptocurrency and Scams* https://consumer.ftc.gov/articles/ what-know-about-cryptocurrency-and-scams

- *Bitcoin and the Predictability of Crypto Market Cycles* https://www.coindesk.com/ markets/2023/12/06/bitcoin-and-the-predictability-of-crypto-market-cycles/

- *The Impact of Global Events on Cryptocurrency Valuations* https://zenledger.io/blog/the-impact-of-global-events-on-cryptocurrency-valuations/

- *12 Bitcoin Success Stories: Meet Bitcoin Millionaires* https://www.cointree.com/learn/bitcoin-success-stories/

- *Crypto Technical Analysis: Techniques, Indicators, and ...* https://onetrading.com/blogs/crypto-technical-analysis-techniques-indicators-and-applications

- *What Is Bitcoin Mining?* https://www.investopedia.com/terms/b/bitcoin-mining.asp

- *What Is the Bitcoin Hashrate and Why Does It Matter?* https://unchainedcrypto.com/what-is-the-bitcoin-hashrate/

- *Lightning Network: What It Is and How It Works* https://www.investopedia.com/terms/l/lightning-network.asp

- *What is the Future of Blockchain and Cryptocurrencies* https://online.stanford.edu/future-blockchain-and-cryptocurrencies

- *Countries Where Bitcoin Is Legal and Illegal* https://www.investopedia.com/articles/forex/041515/countries-where-bitcoin-legal-illegal.asp

- *How Does The SEC Regulate Crypto?* https://www.forbes.com/advisor/investing/cryptocurrency/sec-crypto-regulation/

- *Crypto Wrestles With Legal Issues, Scoring A Few Key Victories in 2023* https://www.forbes.com/sites/digital-assets/2023/12/27/crypto-wrestles-with-legal-issues-scoring-a-few-key-victories-in-2023/

- *Bitcoin Security: Here's What Makes The OG Blockchain Safer Than Fort Knox* https://finimize.com/content/bitcoin-security-heres-what-makes-the-og-blockchain-safer-than-fort-knox-with-ledger

- *What To Know About Cryptocurrency and Scams* https://consumer.ftc.gov/articles/what-know-about-cryptocurrency-and-scams

- *Cryptocurrency Security: Best Practices for Protecting Your ...* https://cardsrealm.com/en-us/articles/cryptocurrency-security-best-practices-for-protecting-your-investments

- *What is the Future of Blockchain and Cryptocurrencies* https://online.stanford.edu/future-blockchain-and-cryptocurrencies

- *Bitcoin Adoption: Number of Merchants Accepting BTC Payments 2023* https://www.coinspeaker.com/bitcoin-adoption-btc-payments-2023/

- *Case Study: Should We Embrace Crypto?* https://hbr.org/2021/11/case-study-should-we-embrace-crypto

- *Why Bitcoin Mining Might Actually Be Great For Sustainability* https://www.forbes.com/sites/digital-assets/2023/09/21/why-bitcoin-mining-might-actually-be-great-for-sustainability/

- *Cryptocurrency Adoption in Developing Countries* https://www.bitstamp.net/learn/crypto-101/cryptocurrency-adoption-in-developing-countries/

- *The Impact of Cryptocurrency on Traditional Banking* https://www.financemagnates.com/thought-leadership/the-impact-of-cryptocurrency-on-traditional-banking/

- *Open-source Bitcoin education aims to spread global financial literacy* https://cointelegraph.com/news/open-source-bitcoin-education-global-financial-literacy

- *Cryptocurrency Regulations Around the World* https://www.investopedia.com/cryptocurrency-regulations-around-the-world-5202122

- *The Future of Bitcoin Beyond 2024: Challenges and ...* https://aibc.world/learn-crypto-hub/future-of-bitcoin/

- *Bitcoin Scalability: Challenges and Solutions* https://crypto.com/university/bitcoin-scalability

- *UN Study Reveals the Hidden Environmental Impacts of ...* https://unu.edu/press-release/un-study-reveals-hidden-environmental-impacts-bitcoin-carbon-not-only-harmful-product

- *Bitcoin Price Prediction In 2024: Boom Or Bust?* https://www.forbes.com/advisor/investing/cryptocurrency/bitcoin-price-prediction-2024/

www.ingramcontent.com/pod-product-compliance
Lightning Source LLC
Chambersburg PA
CBHW071703210326
41597CB00017B/2316